Children's
Creative Spelling

International Library of Psychology

General editor: Max Coltheart
Professor of Psychology, University of London

Children's Creative Spelling

Charles Read

Routledge & Kegan Paul
London, Boston and Henley

First published in 1986
by Routledge & Kegan Paul plc

14 Leicester Square, London WC2H 7PH, England

9 Park Street, Boston, Mass. 02108, USA and

Broadway House, Newtown Road,
Henley on Thames, Oxon RG9 1EN, England

Set in Baskerville 10/12pt
by Columns of Reading
and printed in Great Britain
by Billing and Sons Ltd.
Worcester

Library of Congress Cataloging in Publication Data

Read, Charles, 1940–

Children's creative spelling.
(International library of psychology)
Bibliography: p.
Includes index.
1. English language – Orthography and spelling – Study
and teaching (Elementary)   I. Title.   II. Series.
LB1574.R38   1985   372.6'32   85-2206

ISBN 0-7100-9802-2
British Library CIP Data also available

Contents

Preface

I Overview

— over

This book is about phonetic influences on children's beginning spelling. In it, we apply phonetics, phonology and the study of writing systems to the understanding of how spelling develops. We are not directly concerned with the teaching of spelling or the development of spelling beyond the primary grades, although both of those topics are touched upon. We do not deal with spelling by disabled learners, second-language learners or adults, although we hope that readers will find ideas here that can be applied to those concerns. The book presents a certain view of how spelling *purpose* develops in the early stages and the linguistic reasons for that development. We hope the book will be of interest to both researchers and teachers in linguistics, psychology, and education. The discussion involves phonetics, phonology, writing systems, language development, dialectology and cognitive and developmental psychology. In order to reach a diverse audience, we have tried not to use technical terms unnecessarily, but we cannot avoid phonetic transcription and terminology. A key to the phonetic transcriptions is provided in Appendix I. It necessarily represents only one dialect, a dialect of American English spoken by many of the children whose spellings are cited.

The topic is important for practical reasons, ultimately. As we have tried to show, children's first efforts in spelling are strongly influenced by speech sounds and relationships among speech sounds that most adults are not aware of. Therefore, some quite frequent patterns in beginning spelling look bizarre but reflect phonetic judgments that have a genuine physical basis. We cannot of course plan or conduct instruction properly if we do not understand these judgments. The situation is roughly analogous to teaching reading without being able to see some of what the student sees.

The work is also important for scholarly reasons only indirectly related to education. What we and other researchers are now doing is treating spelling performance as one window on the development of language and cognition. Through that window we can get a glimpse of how children conceive of the sound system and the writing system of their language. It is perhaps no more than a glimpse; there is a great deal that we cannot see through spelling, and no window is completely undistorted. But spellings do show us that children at certain stages of language development perceive certain sounds as related, and certain relationships as more salient than competing ones. There are not many other ways of getting that kind of evidence.

Compared with the vast research on reading, the study of spelling has been relatively neglected, perhaps partly because it has seemed that spelling is largely an uncomplicated (if occasionally difficult) process of memorization and recall. While various kinds of memory obviously play important roles, the children's spellings show that even spelling involves segmentation, categorization and other cognitive processes applied to language. At least some young children seem to construct (in the Piagetian sense) a spelling system for their language, based on the speech sounds and a partial knowledge of letter names and standard spelling. As Chapter 5 argues, it is entirely plausible that children would begin with representations at the level of speech sounds. To see the problem from their point of view, we must imagine what it is like to have had experience with the spoken language only. We must then comprehend the differences between children's spelling and the standard system, which represents larger units as well as speech sounds. The differences between these two systems define what children must learn (but not how they can learn it).

The work described in this book is also distinguished by its data: spelling errors are the primary data, not because they constitute failures of learning or teaching, but because they give us clues to children's judgments. Standard spellings cannot do that; we can never be sure that a standard spelling does not come from memory, copying or direct instruction, i.e., processes which do not tell us much about children's knowledge of language. But we can be almost certain that a nonstandard spelling of an everyday word did not come directly from print or from an adult, so we can make inferences about the child's contribution. As we have discussed in Chapter 2, spelling errors have long been the primary data for educational research on spelling, but for a different reason from ours, namely that errors help to identify difficulties which may then be corrected. Naturally, we want to ease the burden of learning to spell; in English, at least, it takes large amounts of time in school, and spelling difficulty or disability hinders large numbers of otherwise highly competent people all their lives. But our interest in spelling errors (hereafter called nonstandard spellings) arises first because they are evidence of basic knowledge and processes.

This book is a synthesis; its aim is to pull together the work of the last decade on phonetic influences on beginning spelling. Little of the research reported here is our original work, but most of it has been previously unpublished, or published only in inaccessible forms, such as dissertations and local project reports. Some of it was published in languages other than English. The work has been international, and almost none of it was done with a full awareness of related work. For that reason, we have tried to synthesize as well as summarize.

A special concern has been to examine the effects of sound systems and writing systems by looking at languages other than English and dialects other than what is vaguely called 'Standard English.' One theme is that spelling patterns that were first observed among Boston preschoolers (Read, 1970, 1971) are also frequent in the primary grades and in other dialects and other languages (Chapters 2, 3 and 4, respectively).

While these observations are gratifying, we are looking for more than just confirmation. The fact that similar (and sometimes modified) patterns occur with various ages, sound systems and spelling systems tells us more about the processes. With this range of research to look at, we have occasionally been able to draw inferences that were not available to the original researchers. Our other goals have been to identify key research questions, to criticize the research and suggest improvements, to confront one study with another, and finally (in Chapter 5) to outline a general conception of spelling development, or at least parts of one.

This process has not been without its difficulties and shortcomings. The research reviewed, spanning the Atlantic in space and more than a decade in time, is uneven in its goals, its concepts, its terminology and its quality. Some has been more pedagogical, some more psycholinguistic, for example. Even in mundane matters like the names used to designate various speech sounds, there has been anarchy. 'Short,' 'checked,' 'lax,' and 'non-name' have all been used to refer to overlapping sets of English vowels. We have probably committed errors in interpreting this diverse material. As for our own phonetic terminology, we used one set of linguistically-accepted terms consistently (we hope), except in direct quotations. For phonetic symbols, we have used one version of the International Phonetic Alphabet, with adjustments to the language in question. The transcriptions are only as narrow (detailed) as they need to be to represent what young spellers are doing. A revealing fact about beginning spelling is that the resulting transcriptions vary from quite broad to moderately narrow, i.e., from making only basic distinctions to making some fine ones. We have continued the convention of reproducing children's spellings in all-upper case, and standard spellings in lower case.

II Acknowledgments

Many people and at least two institutions have contributed to this work. The main people are Lyda Ruyter, who wrote original drafts of Chapters 2 and 3; Mary Tait, who drafted Chapter 1 and part of Chapter 5; and Nilgun Tolek, who extensively revised Chapter 3 and wrote part of Chapter 5. As the work evolved over two years, the original drafts were all extensively revised or rewritten, so these three graduate students are not responsible for the final versions. Linnea Johnson and Catherine Jarvis helped to locate and keep track of references; Louise Smalley and Dorothy Egener helped to produce finished copy. We are also greatly indebted to the researchers whose work is reviewed here. Though far-flung and diverse, they have formed a chain of description and inference which has begun to lead toward an understanding of how spelling develops.

Chapter 1 is based mainly on Read (1975). For permission to republish tables and figures from that book, I am grateful to the

National Council of Teachers of English.

The writing of this monograph was funded by the Wisconsin Center for Education Research, which is supported in part by a grant from the National Institute of Education (Grant No. NIE-G-81-0009). The opinions expressed in the book do not necessarily reflect the position, policy or endorsement of the National Institute of Education.

1 Creative beginning spelling

One thesis of this book, and of this chapter in particular, is that children's beginning spelling is essentially phonetic. To a greater extent than adults or older children, young children spell by representing speech sounds individually rather than by learning the spellings of whole words or morphemes (meaningful parts of words). Partly because of this focus on sounds, children's spelling is influenced by details of pronunciation and by similarities among speech sounds. This spelling strategy leads to some frequent and typical spelling patterns which appear bizarre to adults (parents and teachers). These are not spellings like *thru* for *through*, but spellings whose phonetic basis is considerably more subtle.

A second thesis is that young children's spelling is essentially creative. Many of the spellings could not have been learned from adults or copied from books, but had to be constructed out of a knowledge of letter names, a conception of standard spelling, and an accurate sense of the sounds that make up spoken language.

The idea that spelling can be creative seems a little odd to most of us: 'creative spelling,' like 'creative table manners,' suggests a mildly anti-social activity. We think of ourselves as either *knowing* a spelling (in some unspecified way), *constructing* a spelling out of known parts, or *looking up* a spelling. But in fact, standardized spelling is a relatively recent development; before the eighteenth century, adults (like children today) seem to have created spellings anew on each occasion, thus writing various spellings of the same word, even of their own names.

I The original data

The phonetic spellings reported in Read (1975) came from a total of thirty-two children in preschools and kindergartens, who created 2517 spellings (tokens) for 1201 words (types). Altogether the corpus included over 11,000 spellings of individual phonemes, which were tallied by phoneme and by the age of the speller. We then conducted some experiments to determine whether kindergarten and first-grade children who are not creating the phonetic spellings really hear the phonetic relations that those spellings appear to represent. It is primarily this observational and experimental evidence that this chapter summarizes, along with a few other studies of preschool spelling.

This analysis is somewhat like error analysis in second-language learning or miscue analysis in reading; we focus on *non*standard spellings. The logic is that children probably do not learn nonstandard spellings from adults or copy them from printed matter. In number, in consistency, and in quality, these spelling patterns are not at all like copying errors. Therefore, children probably create most nonstandard spellings, so that these provide a window on their spelling processes, their notions of writing, and (it turns out) their judgments of speech sounds. What is really remarkable is that different children independently created the same spelling patterns.

II The nature of spelling

English spelling represents the language on more than one level. Some spellings represent phonemes unambiguously according to straightforward correspondence rules; *sin* is such a spelling, as is *sine*, given the convention that a final *-e* after a single consonant indicates that the preceding vowel is 'long.' Other spellings represent morphemes (units of meaning), rather than sounds; thus *sign* is only partly a direct representation of sounds, but it indicates a relationship in meaning and derivation to *signature* and *signify*. The phonemic spellings are often called 'regular' and the morphemic ones 'irregular,' but in fact both are essential parts of the English spelling system (Venezky, 1967, 1970; Chomsky, 1970; Klima, 1972). Spellings have still other functions which require that they not be entirely predictable from phonemes alone, such as distinguishing homophones (*sine/sign*; *rite/right/write*).

Despite these multiple levels of representation, we believe, with Gleitman and Rozin (1977), that unlike the writing system of Chinese, English spelling is fundamentally alphabetic and represents phonemes rather than morphemes, especially for children learning to write. We teach them that way, most words in their vocabularies are spelled that way, and their preschool creative spelling shows that they approach it that way.

Any alphabetic spelling system is fundamentally an exercise in segmenting and categorizing speech, which is physically continuous and infinitely varied. In the 1970s most of the theoretical discussion of spelling concerned the nature of the phonemes represented and their level of abstraction from phonetic (ultimately physical) reality (Chomsky and Halle, 1968; Chomsky, 1970; Klima, 1972). Previously, discussion had taken for granted the nature of the phonemes, focussing on the problem of *which* phonemes are represented (e.g., which dialects) and by what correspondence rules.

Besides this fundamental categorization problem which is inherent in any spelling, writing English with the Roman alphabet creates a categorization problem on another level, namely that of how phonemes are to be grouped for spelling purposes, since by anyone's count there are approximately twenty more phonemes than there are letters in the alphabet. We must therefore spell distinct sounds (again, by anyone's definition) with the same letters, creating spellings whose interpretation depends on their context. The relevant context may be immediately contiguous, as in digraphic spellings like *ch* or *ea*, non-contiguous but still within the word, as with the conventional final 'silent' *-e*, or outside the word (syntactic, semantic and pragmatic), as in *lead* as a noun or verb.

III Children's spelling patterns

A Vowels

Learning to spell vowels presents these basic problems of segmentation and categorization in their most difficult form, perhaps. Vowels are continuous with, and heavily influenced by, neighboring sounds, so it is not obvious how or whether they can be isolated. Vowels vary in infinitely small steps from one speaker to another and one context to another, so it is not obvious how they should be categorized. In English specifically, there are about fifteen phonemically distinct vowels to be represented but only five letters generally used for the purpose. For all these reasons, young children creating their own spellings must group distinct vowels together; their decisions turn out to be interesting.

Children generally spell vowels with only A, E, I, O, U and Y, that is, with these letters singly or in combination with each other or with a following W. These are of course the letters used to represent vowels in standard spelling; they are also the only letters whose names in English contain only vowels and glides (no consonants). Children's selection of these letters may be based partly on the letter names as well as on the standard spellings.

What is interesting, however, is that in order to maintain this distinction, almost never using consonant spellings for vowels or vice-versa, children must (unconsciously) distinguish these two kinds of speech sounds. Adults might use distinct spellings for consonants and vowels simply by having learned standard spellings, but since young children do not generally produce standard spellings, they must maintain the distinction themselves. For example, a child searching the alphabet for a letter whose name contains /u/ as in *boot* might have found Q; a child looking for a way to spell /e/ as in *bait* might have chosen H, J or K. In fact, no such spellings occurred in the Read (1975) corpus, even though most spellings of these vowels were nonstandard. Thus the very fact that vowel spellings are distinct from consonant spellings indicates one basic categorization.

1 Letter-name vowels

Children's spellings do reflect letter names, however, especially for the 'long' or 'tense' vowels that are the names of A, E, I, O and U (phonetically /e/, /i/, /ai/, /o/ and /ju/). By far the most frequent spelling of each of these vowels was simply the letter that it names; Table 1.1 gives examples, and Appendix II lists all spellings with their frequencies. For instance, from children under age six, 74 per cent of the spellings of /e/ were simply the latter A, and 79 per cent of the spellings of /ai/ were simply I, as illustrated in Table 1.1.

Such spellings are almost never exactly standard (because standard spelling uses digraphs like *ea* and the final 'silent' *-e* for these vowels), but they may well have been influenced by standard spelling. Primarily, they illustrate the importance of letter names and help to explain other, more surprising spellings.

TABLE 1.1 *Spellings of letter-name vowels*

FAS	face	LADE	lady	TIGR	tiger
DA	day	EGLE	eagle	LIK	like
KAM	came	FEL	feel	MI	my
TABIL	table	PEBATE	Peabody	TIM	time
NACHR	nature	BREFCAS	briefcase	MISS	mice

GOWT	goat	U	you
POWLEOW	polio	JUNUR	junior
WENDOWS	windows	HUMIN	human
KOK	Coke	FABUARE	February
GOST	ghost	UNITDSATS	United States

2 Other vowels

How, then, do children represent all the other vowels of English, which are not by themselves the names of letters (though some do occur in the names of letters used to spell consonants)? The clearest and most interesting examples are the 'short' or 'lax' front vowels, /I/ as in *bit*, /ɛ/ as in *bet*, and /æ/ as in *bat*.

Consider first the spellings of /I/ as shown in Figure 1.1 for children less than six years old. Two spellings predominate: 65 per cent are I (the standard spelling) and 23 per cent are E. No other spelling occurs more than 5 per cent of the time. It is not remarkable that the standard spelling is most frequent, but why is E so much more frequent than any other nonstandard spelling? In fact, it occurs ten times more often than any other nonstandard spelling except omission. Table 1.2 presents some examples. Moreover, different children created this spelling. Of the twenty-five children who used any nonstandard spellings, twenty-one used E at least as often as all other nonstandard spellings combined; the actual frequencies ranged widely, from 8 per cent to 80 per cent.

We can account for this pattern if we assume that children try to create similar spellings for similar sounds. The vowel closest in

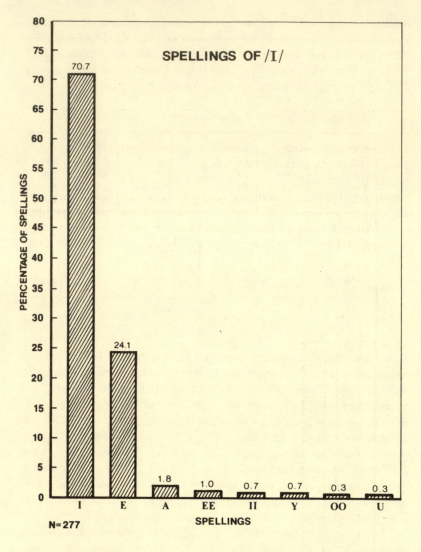

FIGURE 1.1

place of articulation to /I/ is /i/, which is the name of the letter *e*, and *e* is usually part of the standard spelling of this vowel (as in *see* and *sea*). Since these young spellers know the letter names and some standard spellings, when they are uncertain of how to spell

TABLE 1.2   *Spelling of /I/ with* E

SEP	ship	SEK	sink	HEMM	him
FES	fish	WEL	will	DRENK	drink
EGLIOW	igloo	LETL	little	DOEG	doing
FLEPR	Flipper	PEL	pill	SOWEMEG	swimming

/I/, they could create the spelling E simply by spelling it like a similar vowel. As a result, they would spell the vowel of *bit* (as well as that of *beat*) with E.

Now consider the spelling of /ɛ/ by children less than six years old, shown in Figure 1.2. Again, there is one nonstandard spelling more frequent than all others, namely *A*; in fact, for these young children, *A* is more frequent than the standard spelling, *E*, and

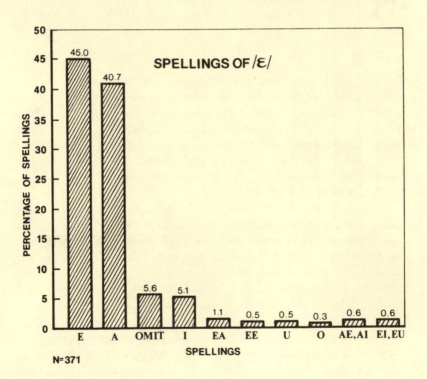

FIGURE 1.2

about five times more frequent than any other nonstandard spelling. Again the question is, why should one nonstandard spelling be much more frequent than all others (indeed all others combined)? Table 1.3 presents examples of this spelling. The assumption that we made above, that children try to spell similar sounds similarly, will also account for this spelling. Phonetically, the vowel of *bet*, /ɛ/, is between that of *bait* and *bat*, both of which children spell A (and the vowel of *bait* is the name of the letter *a*). If children, looking for a way to spell /ɛ/, spelled it like its phonetic neighbors, they would come up with A.

TABLE 1.3   *Spellings of /ɛ/ with* A

PAN	pen	TADDEBAR	teddy bear	SHALF	shelf
FALL	fell	PRTAND	pretend	DAVL	devil
LAFFT	left	RAKRD	record (N)	ANE	any
MAS	mess	ALLS	else	ALRVATA	elevator

Figure 1.3 represents the phonetic relations among the five vowels discussed so far, with lines enclosing the sets which children tend to spell alike. (The phonetic relations are those which phoneticians perceive among these vowels, and which hold between certain acoustic properties; Figure 1.3 does not represent the position of the tongue in articulation, although that has sometimes been claimed. For further discussion, see Ladefoged, 1975, pp. 65-9 and 193-4.)

There are other sets of vowels in English which are related in the same way as those which children tend to spell E and A. For example, the vowels of *boot* and *book* are related in this way, and as we would now expect, children tend to spell them alike. However, these other sets of vowels do not provide clear evidence for or against the hypothesis, because as with *boot* and *book*, standard spelling also sometimes spells them alike. Children could have learned, rather than created, the similarity in spelling. Read (1975, pp. 44-9 and 1980, pp. 123-4) discusses these at greater length.

A bit of additional evidence for the hypothesis comes from older children who have learned the standard spellings of the 'short' vowels, /I/ and /ɛ/. They sometimes *keep* the pairing of short and

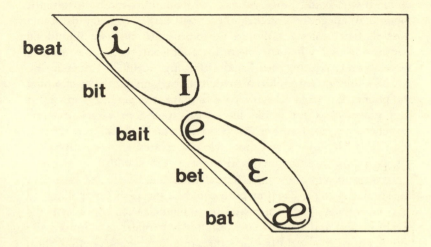

FIGURE 1.3   Phonetic relations among five vowels

long vowels by spelling the long one like the short one, rather than vice-versa. This yields spellings like BRIF for *brief* and BEC for *bake*. With such spellings, children maintain the phonetic pairing by giving up the obvious letter-name spellings with which they began. These spellings are not numerous (just over 7 per cent of the spellings of /i/ and 5 per cent of /e/), but they suggest the force of the phonetic relationship for some children.

3 Experimental evidence
Our hypothesis is that children unconsciously sense the similarity between certain vowels and that some children use this similarity as a guide to creating spellings when they do not know the standard ones. We sought to test the first half of that hypothesis, asking whether children (even those who are not creating their own spelling) do indeed hear the similarities among vowels.

Of course, we cannot directly ask young children whether they think two vowels are similar; even the X:A,B paradigm used with adults ('Is *bed* more like *bayed* or *bid*?') is too abstract for children. The method that worked with kindergarten children involved a puppet named Ed, who liked 'words that sound like Ed.' We began with true rhymes ('Would Ed like *bed* or *bead*?') and then with those children who could judge rhymes consistently, went on to test the pairs that allegedly underlie the creative spellings against other possible pairings, e.g., 'Would Ed like *showed* or *shade*? Would Ed like *aid* or *owed*?' The experiment included controls for the effects of position and meaning; see Read (1975, pp. 120-6) for details.

The kindergarten children made consistent judgments, choosing the phonetically-related pairs to a significant degree. For example, they judged that Ed would like *shade* rather than *showed* and *sad* rather than *sawed*. In other words, young children can perceive that some English vowels are more closely related phonetically than others; vowels are not merely distinct speech sounds.

This result also shows that either the similarity to /e/ (*shade*) or the similarity to /æ/ (*sad*) or both could be the basis for spelling /ɛ/ (*Ed*) with an *A*. We then tested these against each other with the same method and found that the latter is stronger to a marginally significant degree. Adults made the same judgments as children in both experiments, which suggests that they can still perceive the phonetic relations even though they no longer relate them to spelling.

In short, we have observed patterns in children's spelling which can be explained in terms of phonetic similarities, and we have seen that even preschool children can detect these similarities. Moreover, it is difficult to think of other plausible explanations for the spelling patterns, e.g., in terms of visual similarities to standard spelling. Further evidence of the spellings appears at the end of this chapter and in Chapters 2 and 4.

Referring again to Figure 1.3, we can compare the vowels that are phonetically similar (encircled), which children tend to spell alike, with those that are spelled with the same letter in standard spelling (*beat* and *bet*, *bait* and *bat*), and are often linked in teaching (as 'long *e*' and 'short *e*,' for example), although they are not so closely related phonetically.

The basis for the standard spellings is historical; essentially, the pronunciation of 'long' vowels changed without a corresponding change in spelling. As a result, words that have the same root and are therefore related in meaning, such as *serene* and *serenity*, *sane* and *sanity*, typically have their stressed vowels spelled with the same letter, but these meaning relations are evident mainly in poly-syllabic words that derive from Latin, so young children have little basis for recognizing them. As Figure 1.3 suggests, children must reorganize their conceptions of vowels if they begin with the expectation that spelling embodies relations that they can hear and end with a knowledge of standard English spelling.

In both systems, different vowels are spelled with the same letter; the difference is the basis for doing so: perceptual similarities versus meaning relations. In fact, one of the notable characteristics of the young spellers was that they did not hesitate to spell distinct vowels alike. They could have made up new symbols, but instead they did what scribes have done ever since the Greeks adopted the alphabet from the Phoenicians: they extended the symbols they had, to cover the sounds they needed to spell, and they did so on a phonetically justifiable basis.

B *Preconsonantal nasals*

Vowels pose the greatest problem of categorizing sounds in order to make do with the available symbols, but consonants also require some judgments. There are three nasal sounds in English, /m/, /n/ and /ŋ/, the last being the velar nasal at the end of *sing*. In most contexts, children spell the first two nasals in the standard way, using M for /m/, and N for /n/. The velar nasal does not occur in a letter name, and children less than six years old spelled it either N or NG 50 per cent of the time. Both of these can be standard spellings, as in *sink* and *sing*, although N might represent a grouping of /ŋ/ with /n/. Another 26 per cent of the time they spelled the velar nasal G, which (if it is not merely part of an NG spelling) represents its similarity to /g/ (as in *girl*), which is the other voiced velar consonant in English.

Nasals were omitted quite a few times, however: 4 per cent for /m/, 12 per cent for /n/, and 22 per cent for /ŋ/ among children less than six years old. What is really interesting is that almost all of these omissions occur in a particular environment, namely, when the nasal consonant immediately precedes a true consonant (stop or fricative). Table 1.4 presents examples of these omissions. Note in Table 1.4 that nasals before vowels are represented, while those before consonants are omitted, even in the same words (MOSTR, NUBRS). In the total sample (all ages), 24 per cent of /m/s and /n/s were omitted before consonants, but only 1 per cent and 4 per

TABLE 1.4   *Omission of preconsonantal nasals*

BOPY	bumpy	MOSTR	monster	HACC	Hanks
NUBRS	numbers	PLAT	plant	THEKCE	thinks
ATTEPT	attempt	AD	and	AGRE	angry
GRAPO	Grampa	WOTET	want it	SEK	sink
STAPS	stamps	CAT	can't	NOOIGLID	New England

cent respectively, in other contexts. Sixty-three per cent of /ŋ/s were omitted before consonants, but less than 1 per cent elsewhere. Presumably there is a reason for this highly selective omission.

Indeed, nasals before consonants are different from those before vowels, in a way that explains the omission. Nasals in this position tend to be very short, especially when the following consonant is voiceless (Malecot, 1960). The actual difference between *wet* and *went* is primarily in the nasalization of the vowel, rather than in the nasal consonant. The effect is increased in polysyllabic words and after the vowels /I/, /ʌ/ and /æ/. Thus a word such as *anchor* is an extreme case, with possibly no nasal consonant at all, just a nasalized vowel. In other cases, such as *bent*, there may be a residual nasal consonant, but it may be as little as one-tenth the length of that in *Ben*.

This phenomenon means that the children's spellings, omitting just the preconsonantal nasals, are phonetically accurate and based on a reasonable categorization: accurate because they do not represent the nasal where it is very brief or absent, and categorial because, not having any special symbol for the nasalized vowel, they represent it with the same symbol as the oral vowel. In other words, it is only standard spelling which declares that the difference between *bet* and *bent* is a consonant after the vowel; not knowing the spelling, children locate that difference where it really occurs, in the nasalization of the vowel, but then spell that vowel like its non-nasalized counterpart, just as they spell other vowels alike when they lack symbols to distinguish them.

This explanation assumes that children do hear the difference between *bet* and *bent*. Read (1975, p. 57) checked that assumption informally by asking twenty-one kindergarten children individually a series of seven questions like 'If you have a little piece of paper that you can paste onto something else, is it a *sticker* or a *stinker*?' All the children answered all of the questions correctly, and 'they did not hesitate to tell me what I had already suspected – that the task was easy to the point of silliness.'

In support of this explanation is the fact that the omissions increase in just the right contexts. Table 1.5 shows the percentage of nasals omitted after the five vowels that most often preceded a nasal and a consonant. Omissions are most frequent after /I/, /ʌ/, and /æ/, just as Malecot's measurements of duration would predict.

TABLE 1.5   *Preconsonantal nasals omitted following five most frequent vowels*

Preceding vowel	% of nasals omitted
/I/	56.0
/æ/	42.4
/ʌ/	33.3
/ɛ/	26.8
/ə/	18.8

Similarly, Table 1.6 lists the percentage of nasals omitted before voiced and voiceless consonants. Consistently more nasals are omitted before voiceless consonants, where the nasal is likely to be shortest.

TABLE 1.6   *Nasals omitted by voicing of following stop, all ages*

Nasal	% Voiceless	% Voiced	N	Significance of difference
/m/	38	14	38	NS (Fisher)
/n/	27	18	242	NS (χ^2)
/ŋ/	69	53	54	NS (χ^2)
All	35	23	334	$p < .02$, χ^2

On the duration hypothesis alone, however, one might expect *no* omissions of nasals before voiced consonants, since nasals are not generally shorter there. In fact, 23 per cent of nasals in that position were omitted. Read (1975, pp. 56-9) suggests that the relation between the nasal and the following consonant may also encourage omissions. The nasal and consonant are always articulated at the same place (if they are in the same syllable), so that /p/ or /b/ may follow only /m/, /t/ or /d/ may follow only /n/, and /k/ or /g/ may follow only /ŋ/. As a result, there is only one movement of the tongue, i.e., only one articulatory gesture that the speaker can feel. Thus the omission of nasals may have both an auditory and a kinesthetic basis.

1 Experimental evidence

In a series of experiments with first graders, Read (1975, chapter 4) tried to find out whether children in school also omit preconsonantal nasals and what the basis for this pattern is. (Among creative spellers, children older than six do omit these nasals, but not so frequently as younger ones.)

The first task was a simple dictation: thirty-two first graders were asked to spell nine words containing preconsonantal nasals, such as *pump*, *plant* and *rink*. The spellings were scored as 'nasal represented,' 'nasal omitted,' or 'undecidable' (in case the spelling was illegible or the letters contiguous to the nasal were also omitted). Of 275 decidable spellings, 151 (55 per cent) were like POP for *pump*: they represented all of the word except the nasal. This rate is actually higher than that of the younger children, perhaps because the stimulus words had vowels and final consonants most likely to elicit the omissions. Most of the children (twenty-five/thirty-two) were near the two extremes in the number of nasals they omitted: they omitted zero or one, or seven or more. This suggests that the omission is a consistent pattern, as it should be if it is based on a categorial judgment of these sounds.

This experiment was informal and subject to response bias (from having nine words with preconsonantal nasals out of eighteen) and to bias from the experimenter's pronunciation, but it certainly indicates that children in the primary grades also produce this spelling pattern.

The second experiment asked where children think the difference is between *bet* and *bent*. This question distinguishes between the two possible explanations discussed above: if children omit the nasal because it is really a nasalized vowel, they should locate the difference on the vowel; if they omit the nasal because it is articulated at the same place as the following consonant, they should locate the difference at the consonant. That is, if they perceive *bent* (correctly) as [bɛ̃t], then the difference is mainly in the vowel; if they perceive it as having a 'nasalized /t/' at the end, then the difference is in the consonant; and if they perceive it as having a nasal consonant, the difference is between the vowel and the consonant (which would be a puzzling choice from children who do not represent a nasal).

The way Read asked this question was to have a 'Sesame Street' puppet (Ernie) ask the children to spell some words on two small easels with plastic upper-case letters that adhered to the easels. Each easel had a full alphabet (plus extra vowels) arranged alphabetically around its perimeter. Ernie asked the children to spell pairs like *bet* and *bent* (among others), side by side on the two easels.

Eighteen of the twenty-eight children had omitted most of the preconsonantal nasals in a previous spelling task, and as expected, many of them spelled the pairs exactly alike: both *bet* and *bent* as BET or BAT, for instance. In these cases, Ernie looked at the two spellings and pointed to each as he read it aloud: 'bet . . . bent. Gee, that's interesting. They look alike, but they sound different, don't they?' The children almost always acknowledged this homography with no sign of puzzlement or discomfort.

Then the experimenter (in *propria persona*) brought forth a plastic triangle which would adhere either to the easel or to the letters themselves. He said, 'Now here's a special symbol that you can use to show Ernie where the difference in sound is between *bet* and *bent*. You can put it anywhere you want – between the letters or over the letters – to show Ernie where the difference is. Why don't you show Ernie where the difference in sounds comes in *bent*?'

In same manner, the children spelled *sick/sink* and *pup/pump*, interspersed with words that they chose to spell for Ernie. Figure 1.4 shows the three positions of the pointer that bear on the research question.

The twenty-eight subjects fell into three distinct groups. Seven children could not do the task consistently; they did not put the pointer in the same position twice (our criterion for consistency). They made many unscorable responses, such as placing the pointer on or before the initial consonant or simply did not respond. Because of the awareness of segmentation which this task demands, it is not surprising that some first graders cannot respond consistently.

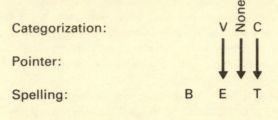

FIGURE 1.4   Possible locations of nasalization in a frequent spelling of *bent*

Ten children, those who represented the nasal on at least two of the three trials, placed the pointer between the vowel and the final consonant (at the nasal, when they represented it). It was *only* these children, who knew the standard spelling, who placed the pointer in this position.

Ten children omitted the nasal in spelling and placed the pointer on or over the vowel, and they did so on all three trials. Only one child placed the marker over the final consonant, and she did so on just two trials. In short, most children who did not know the standard spelling but who chose one position consistently, located the difference at the vowel, which is also phonetically correct.

Some children indicated this judgment quite specifically. They placed the pointer directly on top of the vowel letter or pushed that letter down with the pointer. One girl wrote BAT for both *bet* and *bent*, then placed the pointer over the A, explaining that 'that (A) says [ɛ] and that (A) says [ɛ̃].' Two other children changed the vowel spelling to distinguish the two words, e.g., to SEEK (*sink*) versus SIK (*sick*).

Despite this evidence, might placing the pointer over the vowel be merely the result of a response bias toward the middle of the word? Since the difference in sound does not come at the beginning or end, a child who wrote *pump* with three letters might tend to place the pointer over the middle one. To answer this question, Read (1975, pp. 111-12) replicated the pointer experiment with disyllabic words: *capper/camper, ticker/tinker,* and *crutches/crunches.* In these words, the nasalized vowel is no longer at the center of the word, even in the children's parsimonious spellings. The task is more difficult, so Read chose subjects at the beginning of second grade and illustrated the words in sentences.

Even these second graders represented the nasal on only 30 per cent of the trials, but they were less consistent in where they placed the pointer. Still, those who were consistent placed it on the vowel three times as often as on the consonant. On only five of the sixty trials was it placed in the orthographic center of the word, and no child placed it there consistently. Precisely because of the greater difficulty of the task, one might expect any response bias to emerge clearly, but it did not. So while the replication only weakly supports the hypothesis that children hear the nasalization as a part of the vowel, it tends to disconfirm the idea of a response bias.

In summary, the idea that children perceive preconsonantal nasals as primarily vowel nasalization and for that reason do not spell them, has three independent kinds of support: the spellings, the phonetic facts, and (to some extent) the pointer experiments.

The final experiments involved recorded speech which had been edited with a computer in a phonetics laboratory. First, Read replaced the (brief) nasal consonants in six words like *trunk* with an equal period of silence: [trʌ_k]. He then played these recorded words to twenty-nine first graders and twenty-nine adults, asking them to identify the word that they heard. (On their answer sheets, the adults marked *truck* or *trunk*; the children marked a picture of a truck or one of an elephant's trunk.)

Both groups identified most words as having a nasal: from 62 per cent to 100 per cent of the time, in approximately inverse relation to the duration of the consonant that had been blanked out. This result is like what Malecot (1960) found with adults only, using earlier techniques. There was no difference between the adults and the children.

Finally, Read lengthened the nasal consonants in three words, again by editing digitized speech, and presented these in a spelling dictation task to first graders. The nasal consonants in the original pronunciations of the three words (*can't*, *hunt*, and *mint*) were relatively long (about 60 msec.), and these were doubled in the extended versions. The resulting words, suggested by *hunt*, were noticeably unusual, but readily identifiable. Both the original and extended versions were presented (on consecutive days along with other words, with order of presentation counterbalanced) via headphones to thirty first graders.

There was no difference between the two versions in the frequency with which the nasals were represented. That frequency ranged from 48 per cent to 60 per cent for all the words, except for *can't*, which had an extraordinarily long nasal for that vowel (75 per cent). (The word-final nasals in *game* and *fine* in the same dictation were represented virtually 100 per cent of the time.)

This result seems to argue against a phonetic explanation of the spelling pattern, in that changing the sounds did not affect the spellings. What it may show, however, is that children do not change their spellings immediately upon hearing a new pronunciation; even for first graders, spelling may be more abstract than that. In other words, given a stimulus which is identifiable as a familiar word, a child may represent his or her conception of that word, unaffected by the most recent pronunciation.

On any interpretation, this experiment suggests that teachers are likely to be disappointed if they try to correct children's spelling with exaggerated pronunciation. Confronted with a spelling like HUT for *hunt* – and such spellings appear to be very frequent in first grade – one is tempted to say, 'No, what you wrote is *hut*; the word is *hunt*. Listen: *hunnnt*.' Although this technique may suggest to the child where the problem is, it is not likely to elicit the standard spelling in the first few attempts. The child probably knows what the teacher said, but his (correct) conception of its phonetic form may be changed more readily by seeing the standard spelling than by hearing an exaggerated pronunciation.

Nor should we suggest to a child that she has misheard a word when in fact her conception of it is phonetically correct. It would seem better to say, 'This is how we spell it,' rather than 'This is what it is.' Small differences in wording may suggest a respect for the child's own judgments, where standard spelling is at odds with those judgments. A child who feels that neither the teacher nor the spelling system has any regard for what he can clearly hear may be more likely to develop the despair which some adults feel about English spelling.

As we have seen, children's spelling of words with preconsonantal nasals tends to be consistent, one way or the other. Precisely because these spelling patterns are systematic, no correction is likely to work immediately, but when a child's conception changes, he may change his spelling of many words at once.

C Homography

One result of both the vowel spellings and the omission of preconsonantal nasals is considerable homography: BAT might represent *bat, bet, bait,* or *bent* (and theoretically even the nonwords *bant* and *baint*). In fact, homography is bound to result from representing English with just twenty-four letters (Q and X were rarely used), using primarily single-letter spellings, not digraphs.

That children create homographs by no means shows that they find them desirable; they simply concentrate on representing one sound at a time, without reflecting on whether they have used the same representation for other sounds. Homography is a potential problem for the reader, not the writer, and young writers generally do not concern themselves with their readers. For example, they write messages with no addressee at all or for playmates who they know cannot read.

Nevertheless, children do have other choices: they might rely totally on adult spelling, create digraphs, or even create new symbols. The widespread homography simply shows us the constraints within which they spelled and the way in which they conceived the task.

Of course, homography exists in standard English spelling, too, but it is of a different kind. *A* represents widely different vowels, as in *sane, sanity, father, a* and *small*, and these are partially predictable on various bases. *Sane* and *sanity* are related historically and in meaning; the pronunciation of *small* is predictable from its immediate orthographic context, (the following *-ll*), while *a* is not predictable as a spelling of [ə]. In children's spelling, on the other hand, the homography has nothing to do with meaning relationships or othographic context; it is (partially) predictable from the use of standard spellings in the wrong contexts, as in NAT for *not* and from similarities in sound. In large part, it is these two bases that give children's spelling its distinctive character.

D Initial /tr/ clusters

A third phenomenon in young children's spelling is not nearly so widespread as the vowel spellings or the omission of preconsonantal nasals, and it does not create homography, but like the others, it suggests that children may perceive phonetic properties that their parents and teachers are unaware of. Table 1.7 shows words in which children have used CHR to represent /tr/ at the beginning of a syllable. These spellings are not frequent; these six are the only instances out of thirty-six spellings of initial /tr/, which is itself not very frequent. But once again, a bizarre-looking spelling has a reasonable phonetic basis.

TABLE 1.7　*Spellings of /tr/ with CHR*

AS CHRAY	ashtray	CWNCHRE	country
CHRIBLS	troubles	CHRAC	truck
CHRIE	try	CHAC	track

The /t/ of *trip* is not the same as the /t/ of *tip*. It is *affricated*, i.e., released slowly with a resulting turbulence, like the sound in *chip*, which is essentially /t/ plus /š/ (sh). Thus all three initial sounds are different: that of *tip* is unaffricted (but released sharply, with a puff of air); that of *trip* is affricated and followed by /r/; and that of *chip* is more strongly affricated, and ends with /š/. (There are also small differences in the place at which the tongue touches the roof of the mouth and the shape of the tongue.) In effect, initial /tr/ is between /t/ (*tip*) and /č/ (*chip*) in quality, so we could, with equal justification, spell it with either *t* or *ch*. (We would never use three different spellings because the differences in quality are automatic. To put it another way, since the first sounds of *tip* and *chip* are never followed by /r/, no homography results, whichever spelling we choose.)

The same phonetic process applies to /dr/ clusters (to a lesser extent), and sure enough, a few spellings reflect it: GRADL and JRADL for *dreidel*, and JRAGIN for *dragon*. These spellings might look bizarre to a teacher, parent or even therapist, but they actually reflect accurate perceptions of speech sounds. What a child who spells in this way does not know is that the affrication is automatic and therefore ignored in spelling.

1 Experiments

The spellings alone cannot answer certain questions, however:

– Might other children judge that /tr/ is more like /č/ than like /t/, apart from spelling?

– Might younger children, uninfluenced by standard spelling, make this judgment?

– Do children classify /tr/ with either /t/ or /č/ merely because they lack a distinct spelling for it? Given an opportunity, might they make the narrowest judgment, that all three sounds are different?

To answer these questions, Read (1975) conducted a series of experiments in which kindergarten, first-grade and preschool children were asked to judge which words in a set 'start with the same sound' as *truck* and *dragon*. He first tested the children for their ability to judge sameness of initial sounds, using both the relevant section of a standard reading readiness test and an ad hoc test like the experimental tasks (described below). With these pretests, he selected a sample of forty-nine kindergarten children who could reliably identify words that begin with the same sound, namely /b/ followed by a vowel.

The experimental task used a large card with pictures of eleven objects whose names begin with /tr/, /č/ or /t/. The children first named each object (e.g., *train*, *chair*, *tie*) and then named the keyword picture (a truck). They were then asked to 'find any things here [on the card] that begin with the same sound as that [the truck].' With this wording, the experimenter did not have to pronounce the names of the objects or the keyword, avoiding a possible bias. The task for /dr/ was the same, except that there were fourteen pictures of objects whose names begin with /dr/, /ǰ/ or /d/ (e.g., *dress*, *jacks* and *duck*), and the keyword was *dragon*.

Thirty-six of the forty-nine children made consistent choices on the /tr/ task, meaning those who chose only words with /tr/, only words with /č/ or /tr/, or only words with /t/ or /tr/, with no more than one inconsistency. By the same criterion, thirty were consistent on the /dr/ task. Table 1.8 shows the percentage of these consistent children who chose each type of word.

This task is not an easy one for kindergarten children; even some of the forty-nine who passed the pretests were inconsistent in the experiment. However, most of the children represented in Table 1.8 were quite confident of their judgments, those who chose /č/ words no less than the others. Some children made it clear that they heard an obvious relation between, say, *truck* and *chicken* and

TABLE 1.8 *Percentage of consistent judgments of [tr] and [dr], kindergarten*

Test	Affricate	[tr] [dr] only	Stop
[tr] (n = 36)	42	22	36
[dr] (n = 30)	43	17	40

no such relation between *truck* and *turtle*. The children who chose /č/ and /ǰ/ had performed as well as the others on the pretests of judging sameness of initial sounds.

Moreover, almost all children made the same kind of judgment on both tests: of twenty-nine who were consistent on the two tests separately, twenty-seven chose /č/ and /ǰ/, /tr/ and /dr/, or /t/ and /d/. No child (at any degree of consistency) chose affricates on the one test but stop consonants on the other. This consistency suggests that the tasks are relaible and that the judgments are indeed based on phonetic properties.

In summary, more than 40 per cent of the kindergarten children who could make consistent judgments found that initial /tr/, as in *truck*, begins with the same sound as *chicken*, rather than *turkey*, and similarly for inital /dr/. This is a larger proportion than one would have guessed from the creative spellings. About the same proportion made the opposite judgments, in accord with standard spelling.

The remaining 20 per cent, who made the narrower judgment (that *truck* begins with the same sound as *train* but not *turkey* or *chicken*), may have merely interpreted 'first sound' to refer to the entire initial cluster; their judgment may not have been based on affrication. If these children were trained (on a pretest) to judge only the first consonant in a cluster, or if they were given only two choices (as in spelling) they might readily join one of the other two groups. Therefore, there is no evidence so far that making finer distinctions would help children, for example, that an initial teaching alphabet should provide a special symbol for /tr/, even though many children do perceive that it is different from /t/ followed by a vowel.

a First grade   To see how these judgments develop as children learn to spell, Read gave the same task to twenty-five first graders in the same week. Table 1.9 shows the percentage of children making consistent judgments of each type. Again the two tests agree, but a greater proportion of first graders were consistent in their judgments and, as expected, a greater proportion identified the first sounds of *truck* and *dragon* with /t/ and /d/.

TABLE 1.9   *Percentage of consistent judgments of [tr] and [dr], first grade*

	Affricate	[tr]/[dr] only	Stop
[tr] (n = 17)	29	12	59
[dr] (n = 21)	19	19	62

What is the relation between these judgments and reading experience? The first graders were reading books in a series; those reading the three earliest books made all three kinds of judgments, but none of those in the fourth book or beyond made 'affricate' judgments. One might speculate that words with initial /tr/, like *truck*, were introduced in the third book, but in fact they were introduced in the second. Therefore, there were children who knew how to read *truck* and *chair*, *dragon* and *jacks*, but who still believed that these pairs begin with the same sound; in fact, there were five such children. Obviously children's judgments do not change immediately or necessarily upon learning to read words which represent contrary categorizations. In fact, the creative spellers also typically persisted in their own spellings after they learned to read standard forms; Chapter 5 discusses the implications of this fact.

Read retested these five children individually, showing them three printed words: *train, teddy bear* and *chair*. He asked each child to read these words and then asked if any of the three 'begin with the same sound.' Four of the children picked *train* and *chair* and denied, when asked, that *train* and *teddy bear* begin with the same sound: 'But look,' Read said, pointing to the words, '*train* and *teddy bear* begin with the same letter.' 'Oh, yeah,' one of them assured him, 'but that's different.' (Read, 1975, p. 54.) Obviously these children made judgments of phonetic similarities, had accepted the fact that spelling does not always correspond to these judgments, and were confident enough to resist the implication that their judgments should correspond to spelling.

This independent attitude is appropriate for learning English spelling, which does not always correspond to what we hear. It would be a mistake for a teacher (or parent) to insist that *train* and *teddy bear* are spelled alike (at the beginning) because they sound alike. To many children they do not sound alike, for a good phonetic reason, and similarity in sound is not the only basis for spelling, as some first graders have already recognized.

Read also gave the same task to children in nursery schools, but most of them simply could not make the explicit judgment of similarity, not surprisingly. Only thirteen of thirty-six reached the criterion on the pretest, judging identity; just ten of these were consistent in their judgments on the /tr/ test, and eight on the /dr/ test. For comparison, Table 1.10 shows the percentage who made each of the three possible choices consistently, but only those ten and eight children are represented. If these small numbers are representative, they suggest a developmental sequence, with a majority of *affricate* choices in nursery school, an approximately even division in kindergarten, and a majority of *stop* judgments in first grade. Among the nursery schoolers, as among the first graders, there were some who could read the words but who consistently judged that *truck* and *chair*, not *truck* and *teddy bear*, begin with the same sound.

Finally, Read gave the same task to twelve spontaneous spellers, who ranged in age from 5;0 (five years, zero months) to 6;6 with a mean age of 5;9, like the kindergarten sample. Unlike their age-mates, however, all the spontaneous spellers made consistent judgments, and could name the letters, produce the sounds, and write the words. They were aware of their judgments and better able to express them. Table 1.11 shows the percentage of children making each type of judgment. Clearly, the spontaneous spellers performed more like the first graders (Table 1.9) than like other children of their age (Table 1.8). In fact, they were more consistent and explicit than most first graders. Those who made *affricate* judgments were quite certain of them; one girl even resisted her

TABLE 1.10 *Judgments of first sound of* truck, *nursery school*
n = 13
mean age = 5 years, 0 months

Consistency	[č]	[tr]	[t]	All
complete	4	2	2	1
−1	1	1	–	1

Judgments of first sound of dragon, *nursery school*

Consistency	[j]	[dr]	[d]	All
complete	3	2	2	1
−1	–	–	1	2

TABLE 1.11 *Judgments of first sound of* truck, *spontaneous spellers*
n = 12

	[č]	[tr]	[t]	All
complete	2	1	6	2
−1	1	–	–	–

Judgments of first sound of dragon, *spontaneous spellers*

	[j]	[dr]	[d]	All
complete	3	1	7	1
−1	–	–	–	–

mother's complaint that she was 'fooling' (Read, 1975, pp. 97-8).

In summary, some children from nursery school through first grade do judge that the first sounds of *truck* and *dragon* are like those of *chair* and *jacks*, respectively, rather than *turtle* and *duck*. In kindergarten the proportion of children making these two judgments is about the same, and over three years there may be development from the former to the latter. This same judgment is sometimes reflected in children's spelling, but learning to read the standard spelling does not immediately change it. Thus some first graders who can read these words still feel that *truck* sounds like *chair* at the beginning. Children who make up their own spellings behave like others who are slightly older, but they are more consistent and certain in their judgments.

Methodologically, the experimental task was generally successful in eliciting judgments, although it was too difficult for most nursery schoolers and quite a few children in kindergarten and first grade. Some children simply chose *all* of the words as similar in sound; they should have been encouraged to make a choice. The /tr/ and /dr/ tasks were highly consistent with each other; none of the ninety-nine children tested made *affricate* judgments on one and *stop* judgments on the other, even though several days sometimes intervened. This reliability suggests that the judgments do have a phonetic basis. The pretest of ability to recognize identical initial consonants was a good predictor of consistency and correlated well with a standard test of this skill.

Nevertheless, some questions remain. Is there indeed a developmental trend? If so, why do children begin with *affricate* judgments? If not, are the differences across children merely arbitrary? The basic question is, how do a child's linguistic and cognitive abilities interact with the phonetic structure of his or her language when the foundations of literacy are being laid?

b More-like/less-like studies　Read (1975, pp. 100-4) also studied children's judgments of *relative* similarity (more like/less like) between initial /tr/, /t/ and /č/. The children judged which of two real words (e.g., *toes* and *chose*) 'sounds more like' a rhyming nonce word (e.g. /trowz/) 'at the beginning.' This method proved inferior to the judgments of *sameness* of first sound; a similar proportion of first graders made consistent judgments. Nevertheless, it confirmed that some children do relate /tr/ to /č/; Table 1.12 summarizes the choices of subjects in four age groups. The kindergarten children had a slightly different task from the first graders, so these proportions cannot be compared directly. That even two adults made this judgment may be partly because they were instructed to attend to sounds. Still, the adults' judgments differed significantly from those of the first graders (p. < .001).

Some other conclusions of the earlier studies were also

TABLE 1.12   *Judgments of /tr/*

Grade	N	Mean Age	Consistent Individuals		Overall Percentage	
			/t/	/č/	/t/	/č/
Kdg	25	6,0	15	6	71	29
1	25	6,8	5	6	45	55
2	24	7,10	4	3	49	51
Adult	13	–	9	2	79	21

confirmed: some children judged /tr/ to be like /č/ even though they knew the standard spelling, and again there was only an indirect relation to reading experience. There was no obvious relation to pronunciation: only four of the 168 first-grade pronunciations of the nonce words were [tšr] instead of [tr]. In a study of articulation errors, Venezky (1971) also found that this substitution is infrequent. Nor did the children's judgments relate to *degrees* of affrication (intensity and duration, measured spectrographically) in the /tr/ stimuli. These non-effects simply show that the judgment of /tr/ is really a categorial one, not a direct reflection of pronunciation.

Comparing these latter studies with the former ones, we find that children's judgments of relative similarity (more like/less like) are less consistent than judgments of sameness. Kindergarten children can make more consistent relative judgments of phonemically distinct vowels (above) than of these consonants which do not contrast phonemically. Even so, the relative judgments help to confirm the basic result: that young children do hear the affricated [t] in a /tr/ cluster as similar to /č/; this judgment influences some children's spelling and does not necessarily disappear as soon as the child learns the standard spelling.

E Retroflex vowels and syllabic sonorants

Some other spelling patterns reported in Read (1975) have not been followed up in experiments or other studies of spelling (Chapters 2 to 4), but they do reveal more about the nature of beginning spelling. One of these is children's spelling of retroflex vowels, like the sound at the end of *teacher*. This is not a vowel followed by /r/, as the spelling suggests, but a vowel articulated *together with* (at the same time as) the tongue shape which is charateristic of /r/. Thus a question arises: should it be represented as a vowel, an /r/, or (as in standard spelling) a sequence? Children usually represent it simply R, as in MUTHR and ROBR. About 60 per cent of the spellings by young children are R; 24 per cent are the standard -*er*. The stressed counterpart to this sound is spelled this way 75 per cent of the time, as in BRD for *bird* and GRL for *girl*.

Thus children appear to classify these retroflex vowels as a kind of /r/, distinct from other vowels. This agrees with a study of adults' judgments of similarity, in which these vowels were set apart from all other English vowels (Singh and Woods, 1971). Children do not represent a vowel in every syllable, as standard spelling does.

Somewhat similarly, children represent syllables that consist of an unstressed vowel plus /l/ or /n/ with just L or N, as shown in Table 1.13. The similarity is not exact; in most such words, there is usually no vowel in actual pronunciation, so that the children's spelling is simply phonetically accurate. That is, when a sonorant like /l/ or /n/ follows a consonant, especially one articulated at the same position (such as /t/, /d/ or /s/), there is usually no intervening vowel. Thus *little* is usually pronounced [lIdl], and children often spell it LIDL or LITL.

TABLE 1.13   *Spellings of syllabic sonorants*

LITL	little	OPN	open
CANDL	candle	WAGN	wagon
PEPLL	people	EVN	even
GOBL	gobble	KITN	kitten
PESL	pencil	DEDNT	didn't
SPESHL	special	SATNS	sentence
		SODNLY	suddenly

With these spellings, children distinguish syllables that actually have a vowel from those that do not; when an unstressed 'reduced' vowel precedes a stop consonant (which cannot be syllabic), children usually represent the vowel, most often with I or E: IGAN (again), MINETS (minutes), but sometimes with other letters: UKLOK (o'clock), UPON (upon), AFISHILL (official). Thus the spelling of sonorants gives additional evidence that children have a distinct category for vowels (as opposed to just 'syllable'). This fits with the distinctness of their vowel spellings (see p. 4).

This spelling pattern is particularly persistent. It is actually a bit *more* frequent among children older than six than those younger than six. (See the tables in Appendix III.) On a spelling dictation, twenty-one first graders out of forty-seven produced all of the following:

BRATHER (brother) TABL (table) FETHR (feather)

and others produced one or two of these three. Perhaps the pattern is persistent because it is phonetically accurate.

F Intervocalic taps

When a /t/ or /d/ occurs between two vowels, where the first vowel has greater stress than the second, the /t/ or /d/ is actually a brief 'tap' of the tip of the tongue against the alveolar ridge (at the roof of the mouth). Thus 'letter' has not a [t] (let alone two of them), but a brief tap. Because they occur between two voiced sounds (vowels), such taps tend also to be voiced, and children frequently spell them with D, i.e., as a voiced sound. This spelling is not surprising; it is phonetically accurate.

TABLE 1.14   *Spellings of tap as* D

PREDE	pretty	WOODR	water
FIDI	'fighted'	NODESEN	noticing
LADR	letter	BEDR	better
CIDEJCHES	cottage cheese	RIDEN	writing
BODOM	bottom	ADSAVIN	eighty-seven
AODOV	out of	GADICHANS	get a chance

What is more remarkable is that even young children more often spell this sound T, even where *d* is the standard spelling: NOBUTE, NOBTIEE (nobody), PEBATE (Peabody), MITL (middle). Children may learn from adults that these taps are sometimes spelled *t*, but they adopt that standard spelling more quickly than others; for example, in LATR (letter), WATD (waited), and LITL (little), we see the creative spellings of vowels and syllabic sonorants along with the standard (but phonetically inaccurate) spelling of the tap. The following two sections present related examples.

G Past tense and plural endings

Past tense in regular English verbs has three forms: [t] as in *helped*, [d] as in *robbed*, and [əd] as in *wanted*. Which form occurs depends on the preceding sound. As we might (by now) expect, children often begin by spelling this ending phonetically:

TABLE 1.15   *Spellings of past tense*

LAFFT	left	COLD	called	STARTID	started
HALPT	helped	MARED	married	ADDID	added
SWOUPT	swooped	GLOWSD	closed	WATID	waited
GAST	guessed	KILD	killed	WOTID	wanted
LIKT	liked	STAD	stayed	HATID	hated

Children rather quickly drop this three-way distinction and move toward standard spelling, but what is remarkable is that the first step is often to represent both [t] and [d] with D, while continuing to distinguish these from]əd]. Thus we find intermediate spellings like FIXD, WALKD, FINISHD, LOOKD and PEKD (peeked), which are neither phonetically accurate nor standard. As with the intervocalic taps, children quickly learn to ignore the distinction (in voicing) between [t] and [d], but not by adopting standard spelling directly.

A similar pattern applies to plural endings, which also have three forms: [s] as in *caps*, [z] as in *cabs*, and [əz] as in *dishes*. Here again children may begin by spelling the ending phonetically, but quickly move toward standard spelling by writing S for [z]. However, this spelling is not limited to endings; [z] as an inherent segment of a word is also likely to be spelled S. This is probably an effect of standard spelling; *s* is the usual spelling for /z/, except initially, and *z* is the least frequently used letter in modern English spelling (Venezky, 1970, p. 90). However, the effect of standard spelling is indirect; children often create a spelling for /z/, but one which is normally used for /s/, such as C, SS or SE (Table 1.16). Also, young children often write S for /z/ even when most other spellings in the word are created, such as CHRIBLS (troubles), BKOS (because), HARRS (hers), TRCES (turkeys), or CIDEJCHES (cottage cheese). Thus, like the intervocalic taps and the past tense endings, the contrast between [s] and [z] is one that children quickly learn not to represent. (But even younger children do *hear* that contrast (Read, 1975, p. 70).)

TABLE 1.16   *Invented spellings of /z/*

EC	is	DUSSINT	doesn't	COSE	cows
RAISIC	races	IRSS	ears	SASE	says
TETCHERC	teachers	SISE	size	ISE	eyes
EYECINSTIN	Eisenstein	SOO	zoo		

These last three spellings all involve ignoring a contrast in voicing between alveolar consonants. In all three cases, the contrast is partly predictable, but there are many S-spellings for [z] when it is not predictable, too. Standard spelling almost certainly sets the direction for children's spelling, but there are also nonstandard creative spellings, and words in which the standard spelling has been overgeneralized. In general, this contrast is one that children readily learn not to represent, which suggests that voicing in consonants is of relatively low salience for them.

We can now draw some inferences. A pedagogical orthography, such as the initial teaching alphabet (i.t.a.), which introduces a special symbol for [z] sounds that are spelled *s* in standard spelling (as in plurals), would seem to be marking too much phonetic detail, a distinction that children can easily learn not to represent. This is just one example of the fact that we need to understand children's judgments of sounds and spellings before we can decide whether an initial teaching alphabet is justified and if so, which distinctions should be marked.

In her classic study of children's acquisition of morphology, Jean Berko posed an interesting question. Having shown that children can form plurals and past tenses of new words (and thus that they have learned a rule, not merely memorized forms), Berko asks whether the rule is morphological or phonological in nature (1958, p. 173). The creative spellings provide one answer to this question. The children seem to regard the [s]/[z] and [t]/[d] alternants as single forms at the level relevant to spelling, just as adults do. But because they begin by distinguishing these from [əz] and [əd] respectively, the initial basis seems to be phonological rather than morphological.

H The relation between /s/ and /z/: experiments

Read (1975, chapter 6) reports a series of experiments on whether kindergarten and first-grade children do feel that /s/ and /z/ are more closely related than /s/ and /t/ or /s/ and /š/. If so, this judgment could be the basis of the creative spellings. The next question would be whether the judgment is based on the close connection in standard spelling (/z/ is usually spelled *s*) or the predictable alternation between /s/ and /z/ in affixes: plurals, possessives and verb endings.

Two facts are crucial for understanding these experiments. The first is that /š/, the sound usually spelled *sh*, is a single speech sound, not a combination of /s/ plus /h/, as the spelling suggests. The second is that there is no strictly phonetic reason for choosing one of these relations over the others. /s/ differs from /z/, /t/, and /š/ in one basic phonetic feature each. If people feel that one pair is closer than the others, the reason must be psycholinguistic (in some sense): the influence of standard spelling, the predictable alternation, or the judgment that one of these phonetic relations is closer than the other two.

The experiments were like those on relationships among vowels. A puppet likes words that begin (or end) with the same sound as his name; the puppet is named Sid (or Gus). First Read tested whether each child could reliably identify that sound (/s/) as opposed to a more distant one, like /d/: 'would Gus like *need* or *niece*?' (Note that the test items do not all have the same *spelling* as the puppet's name.) When a child reached a criterion on this task, he tested words 'that don't sound *exactly* like *Gus* at the end:' Would Gus like *bills* or *built* [z-t]?

This first experiment compared /s/-/z/ with /s/-/t/. First graders performed the task easily and reliably, quickly reaching criterion on the items with /s/ versus /d/ and continuing to perform well on such items interspersed with the test items. On the test items, they overwhelmingly chose /z/ rather than /t/; 86 per cent in initial position and 94 per cent in final. In final position, the test items included /z/'s that are predictable (as in *bills*) and /z/'s that are not predictable (as in *rise* – cf. *rice*). There was no difference at all between these two types. There was also no apparent effect of spelling: the judgments of *bills* and *fizz* were exactly the same (and most of the children knew these spellings).

Adults made the same judgment on the test of final /s/: of twelve subjects, all chose /z/ rather than /t/ on all six test items. Thus both adults and children feel strongly that /s/ is more like /z/ than it is like /t/. This preference might arise from spelling or alternation (as in plurals), but if so, it has been generalized to all /z/'s, not just those which are spelled *s* or which alternate with /s/.

The second experiment compared /s/-/z/ with /s/-/š/ in the same way. First graders chose /s/-/z/ in final position 71 per cent of the time, but with a difference: the effect of predictability and/or spelling (they were confounded) was nearly significant, with a greater tendency to choose /z/ when it was spelled *s* or alternated with /s/. In initial position, as in *zip* versus *ship* (where /z/ is spelled *z* and contrasts with /s/), the results were reversed: 63 per cent of the choices were for /s/-/š/. The difference between the two positions was statistically significant and might well result from spelling or alternation, especially since all of the first graders knew that /š/ is spelled *sh*, and most spelled initial /z/ Z and final (predictable) /z/ S.

To check the effect of spelling, Read replicated this experiment with kindergarten children. The five children who (on a later spelling test) spelled /š/ with SH or S favored /s/-/š/; the fifteen children who did not spell /š/ that way (many could not spell it at all) favored /s/-/z/. The difference was statistically significant (p. < .02), and the difference between the kindergarten children and the first graders was also significant (p. < .03). On the same test, adults were sharply divided; most consistently chose /s/-/š/, but some (seven of twenty-three) consistently chose /s/-/z/.

In summary, there appears to be a basic tendency to group /s/ with /z/, which helps to account for the spelling of /z/, but this grouping tends to give way to /s/-/š/ when a child learns that /š/ is spelled *sh*. The original grouping *may* arise from the fact that /z/ is often spelled *s* and alternates with /s/ in affixes, but if so, it is generalized to all /z/'s. On the other hand, it may come from the judgment that the phonetic difference (in voicing) between /s/ and /z/ is less salient than that between /s/ and /š/ (in place of articulation). This difference (in voicing of an alveolar consonant) is the one which we saw is often not represented in taps and past tense endings. /s/ and /z/ are also judged to be closer than /s/ and /t/; learning English spelling can only strengthen this judgment.

diff.
of kind.
1st & 1st

   The influence of standard spelling, <u>seen in the difference between kindergarten and first grade</u>, is perhaps surprising, considering that /š/ is spelled *sh*, not just *s*. Evidently children do not regard this digraph as just another arbitrary symbol: they seem to assume that a sound spelled *sh* is 'a kind of /s/,' as a majority of adults did. In one sense, ths assumption is just the bias that <u>spelling introduces into judgments of speech sounds; the same bias may affect the judgments of /s/-/z/</u>. But /s/ and /š/ are less closely related phonologically, historically, and in spelling; when they are related, as in *race-racial*, they are not spelled *sh*. Evidently children are quick to make inferences from spelling, and some of these inferences are better than others.

   <u>The judgment that /s/ and /z/ are closely related leads children toward standard spelling in most cases, but not in all;</u> two (of seventeen) first graders spelled *zip* as SIP, and three spelled *fizz* as FIS. In responding to such spellings, teachers should not insist too strongly on the contrast between [s] and [z], for English spelling rarely honors it. Only certain /z/'s are spelled *z*, and we can probably not explain to first graders which ones they are, except that they include the ones at the beginnings of words. In any case, what the children are doing is not entirely wrong: assuming that some closely-related sounds are spelled alike.

IV The creative spellers

As we shall see, these spelling patterns are by no means limited to the children in Read's (1971, 1975) original sample, but still it is natural to ask who these children were and whether they were unusual in some way. There were thirty-two children in that sample; eleven of them created 87 per cent of the data; four contributed more than 50 per cent. The study began with two children of professors; the recognition that these two children had independently created similar spellings with an apparent phonetic basis was the point of departure. Read found more children who had created or were creating these spellings in local kindergartens and nursery schools, especially Montessori schools, where writing is encouraged and accepted. The sampling was not systematic, and it was biassed toward children of upper-middle-class professional families (but recall that the original Montessori schools were in the slums of Rome).

A key characteristic of these children's homes was the parents' willingness to accept this seemingly bizarre beginning spelling. Even though some parents feared that their child would develop bad spelling 'habits,' they welcomed the child's first writings; provided simple materials, such as alphabet blocks or paper and pencil; and answered basic questions, like 'How do you spell "chuh"?' From parents or siblings, from nursery school, or from children's television, the children learned the names of the letters.

Of course, as Goodman and Altwerger (1981) have pointed out, young children see print and other symbols in many salient contexts, such as food packages and public signs. Parents are not the only, or even necessarily the most important, source of information about the meanings and functions of print. For example, a child who likes a certain restaurant will notice its sign and the letters on it, and may make a connection between those letters and the name of the restaurant. The home and school environment of the children in Read's sample, while relatively privileged, was certainly not unique in displaying print in colorful, salient contexts.

What is notable about the creative spellers is that they obviously solved the segmentation problem readily and then extended their little knowledge of letter names and standard spellings independently. Most of them began to read early, and as C. Chomsky (1971) points out, reading often *follows* the spelling. With this independent and creative start, most of the children used their writing skills in clever ways. One boy, banished to his room as a punishment for having hidden his mother's bracelet, sent a series of increasingly conciliatory messages downstairs on paper missiles, ending with LOOKC IN THE BAC YRD LOOKC BHINE THE SHED. Most of the children wrote little stories or captions on their drawings; some even wrote prayers and poems.

Were these children outstanding in general intelligence? Judging from their later achievements in school, some probably were, but other studies (below and Chapter 2) indicate that the spelling patterns themselves are not limited to exceptional children. The skills necessary for creative beginning spelling may be quite specific to the task, crucially the ability to segment speech into phonemes, which has been shown to be a key difference between children who learn to read easily and those who do not (Zifcak, 1977; Liberman, Liberman, Mattingly and Shankweiler, 1980).

Two parent/researchers have even described the very first creative spellings of their children. C. Chomsky (1971) recalls that her son, playing with plastic letters, put together KT and called it *Kate*, combining the name of the letter *k* with the sound represented by *t*, 'a handy combination of the syllabic principle and the alphabetic principle,' Chomsky notes. G. Bissex (1980) was reading one day, ignoring her son Paul's efforts to get her attention. He 'decided to break through print with print,' writing her his first note: R U D F ('Are you deaf?'). Paul got his mother's attention.

A *Other studies of preschoolers*

Other researchers soon began to look for these spelling patterns. In fact, as early as 1963, Goodman and Goodman had reported on the spelling of a self-taught reader (age 6;5). Among this girl's spellings were WATHER for *weather* and SWAP for *swamp*, but these were not frequent enough to be considered characteristic. Most subsequent studies have been done in the primary grades (Chapter 2).

Paul (1976) followed for one year the development of spelling among the kindergarten children whom she was teaching. She observed the letter-name spellings (BOT for *boat*) and the spelling of syllabic sonorants without a vowel. Her pupils simply did not spell many words with preconsonantal nasals, and they did not pair short vowels with the corresponding long ones, like E for /I/. In fact, Paul did not find much consistency in the spelling of short vowels.

Paul divides the spellings into four stages:

Stage	Characteristics
One	First phoneme only
Two	First and last phonemes, letter-name vowels
Three	Short vowels represented, but inconsistently
Four	Sight vocabulary spelled in standard way; digraphs like *sh*, *ch*, and *th*.

She notes that children are far more interested in the process than in the product of writing, and she recommends that other kindergarten teachers encourage pupils to create their own spellings. Like Chomsky (1971), she feels that

> rather than inhibiting later development of good spelling, allowing children to write on their own in the early stages encourages active involvement and careful thinking about spelling which they spontaneously refine as their knowledge of reading grows (p. 200).

The largest study of creative spelling in preschool is that of Mayhew (1977). To 106 kindergarten children (90 per cent white) of low to middle socioeconomic class in rural Virginia, Mayhew dictated words selected for their phonetic form, in sentence contexts. The children spelled the words with magnetic capital letters. In order to elicit spellings of vowels even from children who tended to represent only initial phonemes, one task consisted of words beginning with vowels; the children were to spell only the first sound, with just the letters *a*, *e*, *i*, *o* and *u* to choose from.

The most striking confirmation of the creative spelling patterns was precisely the one that Paul did not observe, namely the spelling of a short vowel with the letter whose name is phonetically similar (Table 1.17). The creative spellings of /I/ and /a/ were far more frequent than in Read (1975).

TABLE 1.17   *Spellings of lax vowels in Mayhew (1976)*

Vowel	Created	Standard
/ɛ/	A 53%	E 25%
/I/	E 71%	I 11%
/a/	I 38%	A 23%, O 19%

Mayhew also observed many spellings with preconsonantal nasals omitted; only 46 per cent of the children in her sample attempted to represent the medial portions of such words, but those children omitted 86 per cent of the preconsonantal nasals. Among spellings of /tr/, none were CHR, but 18 per cent were H or HR. (Recall that the name of the letter *h* contains /č/.)

Mayhew also looked at the relation between creative spelling and measures of reading knowledge. A knowledge of letter-sound correspondences, reading readiness (as measured by the Metropolitan Reading Readiness Test), and being able to recognize some words on sight all correlated with creative spelling. There was no difference between boys and girls in the frequency of 'phonemically-acceptable' spellings. Eighty-three per cent of these kindergarten children used systematic spelling strategies.

Mayhew describes six stages of spelling development, essentially like Paul's four, focussing on what positions in words are typically represented and how vowels are spelled. Sixty per cent of the children in her sample were in stages two (one phoneme represented, usually the initial one) and three (the initial phoneme and one other represented).

V Conclusion

We have seen that certain patterns of creative spelling occur in preschool and kindergarten. Some of them have also turned up in first grade; Chapter 2 presents more evidence. We have also seen experimental evidence that children who are not creating these spellings nevertheless share the phonetic judgments that underlie them. What precisely is the nature of these spelling patterns, and what is their theoretical and practical significance?

We can look at the spellings in at least three ways. In one sense, they are simply phonetically accurate; for example, GARDN is an accurate representation of *garden* as it is usually pronounced, and BET is an accurate representation of *bent*, given no special symbol for the nasalized vowel. Since children seem to be good at learning phonetic details, e.g., in a second language or dialect, perhaps it is not surprising that their spelling is phonetically accurate, even in unexpected ways.

In another sense, the spellings amount to tacit classifications of speech sounds; as explained above, *all* spelling involves classification. For instance, spelling short vowels like similar long ones (BAT for *bet* and BET for *bit*) seems to depend on the (accurate) judgment that these vowels are closely related. Likewise, CHRIP for *trip* embodies a judgment that the affricated /t/ that precedes /r/ should be classed with /č/ rather than with the /t/ of *tip*. Even the omission of preconsonantal nasals involves classification: the decision to represent the nasalized vowel like the corresponding oral one.

Finally, the spellings give evidence of what phonetic properties are relatively *salient* for children. For example, they quickly learn not always to represent voicing in alveolar consonants (taps, past tenses and plurals), while maintaining other distinctions, such as place of articulation. In short, the spellings reveals both phonetic accuracy and (unconscious) judgments of relatedness and relative salience among phonetic properties; that is their theoretical import.

Studying the phonetic bases of children's spelling complements other ways of studying their phonetic and phonological development. One can study their pronunciation errors (Olmsted, 1971), their perception errors (Graham and House, 1971), their knowledge of phonological rules (Morehead, 1971), or even their explicit judgments, e.g., of rhymes (Knafle, 1973). Each of these yields some notion of how speech sounds are related for children. What we do not yet know is how these studies fit together; for example, do all five tasks draw upon the same set of phonetic relations?

The spelling evidence has its own particular strengths and weaknesses. Perhaps its greatest strength is its face validity; these spellings constitute children's spontaneous efforts toward solving the major educational problem of the early school years, the acquisition of literacy. Even though we have gone on to *elicit* spellings and phonetic judgments, we started from naturalistic data. The fact that the explanations involved phonetic properties that can be demonstrated, measured and manipulated adds to their credibility. When the spellings, the phonetic explanations and the experimental evidence converge, we can have some confidence in the hypotheses.

The weaknesses of the evidence, however, also come from its naturalism. Only a minority of children create some of these spellings spontaneously, such as those of the short vowels. We cannot control factors such as the actual phonetic input to the spelling (what pronunciation, precisely, is the child representing?), the alternative spellings that the child might consider and, of course, the influence of standard spelling. The alphabet and standard orthography limit the set of judgments that we can study through spelling. They pose certain problems, such as how to spell /tr/, while making other decisions obvious, such as how to spell /b/. The spellings suggest that children hear a relation between /ɛ/ (the vowel of *bet*) and /æ/ (the vowel of *bat*), but they suggest nothing about the relation between /i/ and /e/, because these happen to be the names of the letters *e* and *a*. Studies that elicit spellings and other judgments or manipulate sounds can overcome some of these limitations, but there is always a trade-off between face validity and control.

Educationally, the phonetic explanations make it possible for teachers to understand a type of error that they have not previously recognized. Teachers of young children are not surprised to see visual reversals like *rodot* for *robot*; they expect regular spellings to be overgeneralized, like SED for *said*; they often see standard spellings in the wrong position, like CKUP for *cup*. Like these, the creative spellings may look bizarre, but they are based on a reasonable principle: that spelling represents sounds, and that similar sounds may have similar spellings. A child who makes these errors is actually on the right track, in that different sounds *are* spelled alike in standard spelling, but because of historical and morphological relations, not phonetic ones. A teacher should realize that such a child is perceiving words correctly and spelling them reasonably.

Consider CHRAC for *truck*, produced by one of the creative spellers (Douglas) at age 5;4. The final C is a standard spelling for /k/, but not in final position in monosyllables. *A* for /ʌ/ is fairly common in creative spellings (about 10 per cent), possibly because of the frequent word *a*, which, when spoken in isolation, is like the vowel of *truck*. CHR for /tr/ is of another sort, as we have seen. Douglas will not be enlightened by being told that *ch* spells 'chuh,' as in *chicken*. He already knows that; in fact, that is why he writes CH in *truck*. Nor will exaggerated (or exasperated) pronunciation help. A more pertinent and less discouraging correction might be to say, 'Yes, it sounds a little like "chuck" at the beginning, but it also sounds a little like "tuck," and that is why we spell it with a *t*.' To give the right information, a teacher needs to recognize the three different bases of these three nonstandard spellings.

The creative spellings (and experiments) also tell us something about the development of spelling. Like some other recent studies (Chapter 5), they show that the foundations of spelling are laid before first grade. They show that as we might have expected, children begin at a concrete level, namely with speech sounds, and they expect that spelling will reflect what they can hear.

The spellings do not support a common assumption: that children expect each distinctive speech sound (each phoneme) to have a distinct spelling. Such a spelling system (approximated in Dutch, Spanish and Turkish) might be easier for children, but the creative spellers spontaneously use the same spelling for different sounds, perhaps because they consider only one sound at a time as they spell. These creations, together with the early adoption of some standard spellings in which different phonemes are spelled alike, shows at least that we need to investigate what is optimal for beginning spelling, rather than simply making the common assumption, as does the initial teaching alphabet (i.t.a.).

The contrast between concrete (phonetic) spellings at the beginning and rather abstract standard spellings as the target gives us some conception of development. From spelling the vowels of *bet* and *bat* alike because they are similar in sound, children learning English have to move toward spelling *please* and *pleasant* alike, even though they are quite different in sound (but related historically and thus occurring in the same root). The fact that spelling phonetically at first does not appear to hinder this development suggests that learning to spell is not just acquiring habits. Rather, spelling truly *develops*, rather like children's drawing, from representing salient and concrete properties with a few simple strategies to representing more abstract properties with a variety of strategies. Chapter 5 will elaborate on this conception of development.

2 Spelling in the primary grades

As we have seen, some children start spelling on their own before receiving instruction in school and often before learning to read fluently. Although their spelling efforts are creative, many spellings appear bizarre to parents and teachers who do not know that such spellings are common and have a phonetic basis. As a result, some parents are concerned that the spellings represent the beginnings of 'bad habits' and perhaps serious difficulties later. Are some potential early spellers then discouraged from recreating writing for themselves? Evidence is hard to come by, but it seems likely.

Whether or not children attempt spelling at home in play, they must do so later at school in earnest. Then, too, children spell words in distinctly nonstandard ways. It turns out that some patterns of beginning spelling in school are the same as those of the preschool creative spellers. In this chapter we will review the recent research on spelling patterns in the primary grades, especially the patterns discussed in Chapter 1.

Similarities between preschool invented spelling and spelling in primary classrooms are all the more remarkable because of the differences between the two settings. These differences are probably not as great now as they were in 1970, because since then, Carol Chomsky (1971, 1975a, 1975b, 1979), Paul (1976), Gentry and Henderson (1978), Temple, Nathan and Burris (1982), Fox and Allen (1983) and others have suggested ways for primary teachers to expand the opportunities for children to write and have helped teachers to understand and value the nonstandard spellings that result. In quite a few first grades and kindergartens, children are encouraged to write in a variety of activities and settings, with the understanding that their spellings will be accepted, or that standard spelling will be emphasized only in specific lessons or formal contexts. This change has a longer and better-documented history in Great Britain than in the United States (Britton, 1970; Rosen and Rosen, 1973).

Even so, the circumstances in which young children spell vary in important ways; not all primary classrooms in which children's own spelling is accepted are alike, any more than are homes and preschools. Some of the variables are the motivations for writing, the degree of spontaneity vs. elicitation, and the extent to which the child feels that his or her performance will be judged. Others are the freedom to select media, occasions, topics and words. Settings also vary in the extent to which they suggest that reading and writing are related, so that one should be able to read what one writes, and that reading and writing are skills to be mastered, as opposed to natural tools of expression. If some patterns of children's spelling in homes, preschools and primary classrooms are consistent despite these variables, then we have all the more reason to think that these patterns reflect ways in which children apply their knowledge of language to beginning spelling, rather than random guesses or flashes of insight.

I Lists of spelling 'demons'

During the first half of this century, most studies of spelling aimed to identify difficult words and difficult elements of words, usually by compiling lists of errors made by children, either in classroom assignments or in less formal writing. These studies had various shortcomings, such as the failure to control for frequency of occurrence and failure to report in sufficient detail how the data were collected. They have now been generally superseded by research which attempts to predict both the occurrence and the nature of errors by attending to the structure of spellings in greater detail. Cahen, Craun and Johnson (1971) provide a thorough critical survey of research on spelling difficulty.

Outmoded though they are, the compilations of spelling errors from the 1920s and 1930s are still valuable precisely because, given their limited aims, they present, not analyses of spellings, but extensive lists of actual misspellings. These lists provide a valuable test for our theories, unbiased at least in the sense that the data collection could not have been influenced by theories that developed later.

Prominent among these studies (and most extensive) is the work of Arthur Gates (1922, 1926, 1937) and his student James Mendenhall (1930a, 1930b), who helped to conduct Gates's large study of spelling errors. Mendenhall elicited spellings from 100 pupils in grades one through six in New York City, with about 300 to 500 words per grade, for a total of 2300 words. One can sense the goals and content of this work from the conclusions of the article (1930b) which is based upon the monograph (1930a):

1   The most frequent error for a word characterizes 50 per cent of the misspellings for that word. This percentage is high enough to warrant special consideration. [contra Horn, 1919 – CR]
2   In general, the hard spot of a word is either at the center or immediately at the right of center. The initial letters of a short word are no more difficult to spell than the initial letters of a long word.
3   The number of errors in any one letter position is associated with the number in any other position less closely than with the difficulty of the word.
4   In general, the letters occurring most frequently are most often in error. Moreover, some letters 'e,' 'a,' 'i,' and 'u' are associated with error much more frequently than their occurrence warrants.
5   Difficulty is associated with particular letters (singly or combined) more closely than with general aspects of words, such as length, the number of vowels, the number of syllables and the position of the accent.
6   The writer suggests the use of a method of grouping based upon two features of words and their errors: (a) common visual elements and (b) common types of errors. ['Common' here means 'shared,' not 'frequent.' – CR] The efficacy of this method, of course, awaits further experimental investigation. (pp. 655–6)

Without judging the methodology, we can see that this earlier work had serious scientific aims; it has much more to offer than merely a list of spelling errors (although Gates (1937) is primarily such a list). However, the primary goal was to identify the locations of spelling difficulty, rather than to explain that difficulty in terms of spelling processes. In particular, there was little reference to the phonetic characteristics of the words to be spelled. In the appendix to his dissertation, Mendenhall lists most-frequent misspellings, classified as additions, omissions and substitutions. This classification, with variants, has in fact been quite customary in spelling studies. But on phonetic grounds, we know that not all omissions are alike: omitting preconsonantal nasals is different from omitting vowel spellings in representing /əl/, /əm/, and /ən/, and each of these is different from omitting graphemic markers like final 'silent' -e, as in letter-name spellings.

A Post-hoc analysis of Gates

Recently, Temple (personal communication, 1982) has reanalyzed some of the spelling errors reported in Gates (1937) to see if they were like the preschool inventions. In general, he found substantial proportions of such spellings: 28 per cent and 30 per cent of the errors in first and second grade, respectively. This estimate is likely to be conservative because in this unpublished draft, Temple used some overlapping categories, with the result that spellings like the invented ones were in some cases counted as other types.

The core of Gates (1937) is a list of 3,876 words which were presented (in sentence context) to New York City elementary-school pupils to be spelled. For each word, the list indicates the 'hard spots,' the one or two most frequent misspellings, the average grade at which that word was introduced in spelling materials, and the grade at which 40 through 90 per cent of the children (in 10 per cent increments) understood the word, as measured by a multiple-choice vocabulary test. The list also indicates what proportion of the errors were in the 'hard spot(s)' for each word and what proportion of the total errors were the one or two most frequent spellings cited. We have counted the instances in which the most frequent misspelling(s) correspond to one of the preschool spelling patterns described in Chapter 1: for example, BAST as a most-frequent misspelling of *best*. In describing the results of this analysis, when we refer to 'grade four or below,' we mean the average grade placement as reported by Gates. Gates actually presented each ·word in the grade below that at which it was introduced in the spelling curriculum of each school, so a word with an average placement at grade four was presented to third graders on the average, but might have been presented at any grade in a particular school.

For words containing /ɛ/, 55 per cent at grade three or below have most-frequent misspellings with A; those misspellings account for 33 per cent of the errors on those words, on the average. For words containing /I/, 21 per cent at grade three or below have most-frequent misspellings with E, constituting 36 per cent of the errors on those words. For words with preconsonantal nasals, 12 per cent at grade four or below have most-frequent misspellings in which the nasals are omitted, making up 26 per cent of the errors. These figures are probably a conservative reflection of the frequency of the spelling patterns, since Gates cites only the one or two most frequent misspellings. Even on the basis of these published examples, however, we can conclude that spellings like those described in Chapter 1 did occur frequently in the elementary grades approximately forty years before they were identified as having a phonetic basis. (Gates began his study in 1928.)

In summary, the extensive research on spelling from the 1920s and 1930s has provided a wealth of data with some pertinent observations about the positions of spelling errors. Theories of spelling processes and explanations of spelling patterns, however, require accounts of pronunciation, language acquisition, memory and cognitive development which were simply not available then. Whether they are adequate now remains to be seen.

II Current research

Research on children's spelling in school has taken a new course in the last decade or so. The basic difference is that we now consider spelling to be a psycholinguistic performance, to be understood in terms of linguistic and cognitive concepts. Thus we can understand the creative spellings described in Chapter 1 in terms of categorizations of phones and phonemes, based on similarities in phonetic features. If spellings are data to be explained with concepts from psycholinguistic theory, they can also be used to test and modify that theory. For example, the preschool spellings suggest that children sense relationships among phonemes, i.e., that phonemes are not discrete objects in children's phonological space. They also suggest that at about age five, children approach spelling in a rather phonetic manner, possibly because they have only partial knowledge of phonological and morphological structure.

As a result of this conception, pedagogical questions no longer necessarily drive research on spelling. To some extent the research reported in this chapter did grow out of a concern for instruction, but it has also been driven by psycholinguistic questions. For example, some studies use children's spellings as evidence of perceived phonetic similarities, less biassed by a knowledge of standard spelling than the adult judgments that have been used for this purpose. Another consequence of the new conception is that a wider range of data seems pertinent. Spellings created outside of school, children's judgments in tasks other than spelling, and evidence from languages other than English all contribute to current research. Certainly the need to improve the teaching and learning of spelling is one strong motivation for examining children's spelling, but it is no longer the only one. As in the study of language acquisition generally, we now assume that the best way to improve teaching and learning may be to understand the basic developmental processes.

Like earlier research, current investigations still focus on children's spelling 'errors,' but the reason for this focus has changed. We now value nonstandard spellings for what they can tell us about psycholinguistic processes. Standard spellings are of less interest, not because they represent successful instruction, but because they do not indicate how a child arrived at them.

Moreover, not all nonstandard spellings are equal; some patterns develop earlier, some persist longer, some are much more frequent than others. Some nonstandard spellings represent a more advanced conception of the task or the language than others. Occasionally, we can even discern that the same spelling occurs for different reasons, one more advanced than another. Beers, Beers and Grant (1977, p. 239) found that primary children created spellings like GAIT for *gate*, at first because the vowel is a diphthong, but later because they have learned to represent 'long' vowels with digraphs (as in *raid*). The basis shifts from a phonetic one toward the graphemic patterns of standard spelling. Accordingly, even knowing the frequency of particular errors does not tell

us enough; we need to find out *why* children create certain
spellings. Research on reading has taken much the same attitude
and has identified distinct bases for 'miscues' (Goodman, 1969;
Goodman and Burke, 1972).

The prevailing attitude toward standard English spelling has
also changed in the last decade. Previously, it was considered to
represent the language at approximately the level of the phoneme,
but in a very irregular manner. Venezky (1967, 1970) showed that
pronunciation is generally predictable from English spelling,
provided that three levels of representation are all considered. The
first is the correspondence between sounds (phonemes) and
spellings. Each spelling, especially of consonants, can be pronounced in only a few ways. The second level is that of the
morpheme; a morpheme tends to have the same spelling in various
contexts, even if its pronunciation changes. An often-cited example
is the past-tense and participial suffix –ed; it has three pronunciations, depending on the preceding sound, but only one
spelling. The third level is not really a level of representation but a
set of graphemic (spelling) conventions, such as the rules of
capitalization and the use of orthographic markers such as -*e* after
a single consonant to mark the quality of a preceding vowel (e.g.,
rid versus *ride*). Chomsky and Halle (1968) and Carol Chomsky
(1970) also contributed to the reassessment of English spelling,
emphasizing its morphophonemic consistency.

The predictability which Venezky demonstrates is from spelling
to pronunciation, however; given *e*, *ea*, *ee*, or *eCe* in context, a
reader can predict the vowel /i/, usually correctly. It has not been
shown that a writer can predict the spelling of /i/ as consistently.
However, the change in attitude toward English orthography has
affected research on spelling as well as reading in at least two ways.
It has helped us to distinguish levels of representation and has
shown that some apparently irregular spellings are actually regular
at a deeper level.

A Fisher

One of the first to observe phonetic spellings in the first grade was
Fisher (1973). She classified the spelling errors of seventy-five first
graders in a Maryland classroom, where the reading instruction

was of the 'language experience' type. In the analysis, Fisher divided the children into three groups on the basis of the number of words that they had produced in their writing. She classified errors primarily as name vs. non-name vowels, voiced vs. voiceless consonants, and substitutions vs. omissions. She was not, therefore, in a position to report on every variety of invented spelling. She was looking for differences in the frequency of substitutions and omissions across the three groups; by and large, she did not find them. She did find some of the invented spellings, however: A for /ɛ/ made up more than half of the errors for /ɛ/ among the high and middle groups. Moreover, the children used A for /ɛ/ much more frequently than they used A in any other nonstandard spelling for a lax vowel. In the low group, E was the most frequent nonstandard spelling for /I/, although I (not A) was the most frequent nonstandard spelling for /ɛ/. One of Fisher's conclusions was that the spellings of both name and non-name vowels fit predictions based on Read (1971).

B Gerritz

Gerritz (1974) also examined first-grade spelling development, specifically looking for the invented spellings. She studied the spellings of vowels (only) in journals written by twelve first graders throughout the school year. Because Gerritz was the teacher in that classroom, she could observe development in detail and in relation to reading instruction. In Chapter 5 we will report her observations on the effect of reading instruction, the consequences of extensive opportunities for writing, and the long-term effects of early nonstandard spelling.

Gerritz found, not surprisingly, that her first graders produced many more standard spellings than the preschoolers described by Read (1971) and more of the spellings that Read had found among the older children in his sample. Gerritz summarizes her results in this way:

> Did the spellings used by the children in this study correspond to those found by Read in his preschool study? Yes and no depending on the position and kind of vowel. The children did use the same spellings, as those Read found for the front lax and

the back unrounded [/a,ε,I/ – CR] vowels. For all other categories, the children tended to add spellings of their own, or not to use the Read spellings at all. Children did, however, pair tense and lax vowels, as Read suggested they would: seven of the twelve students paired at least one set of vowels.

What phonological knowledge is indicated by first graders' spelling of vowels? Three findings are of interest here. First, the children did pair the tense and lax forms of the front vowels, indicating that they were aware of the components that each member of the pair had in common. In doing this, the children were confirming not only Read's first finding, but also his second suggestion, based on limited evidence, that the pairs changed in spelling but were preserved even after some children learned to read. Second, the children appear to have distinguished between the front vowels and all of the other vowels. Third, the children appeared to have a sense of the presence or absence of glides [because they used W and Y to represent the off-glide in diphthongs] . . . . These three findings are an indication that young children to some extent are basing their spelling on the components of the vowels themselves (pp. 96-7).

Gerritz found that for [I] and [ε] the most frequent spellings were the standard ones (I and E respectively) at 82 per cent and 64 per cent. But by far the most frequent nonstandard spellings were the 'invented' ones (E and A respectively) at 9 per cent and 17 per cent. Gerritz encountered the same problem that Read did in studying back rounded vowels: there were fewer tokens of them and the spellings overlapped with standard spelling so that she could not say what was invented and what was standard spelling but in the wrong context. Gerritz's observations tend to confirm that backness is more salient than height: that children distinguish front vowels from back vowels more sharply than they distinguish vowels that differ in height.

C Beers and Gentry

Several students at the University of Virginia have written dissertations on spelling, under the direction of Edmund H. Henderson. These students have shared a concern for the development of spelling in the primary grades in relation to word knowledge and general cognitive growth. The work has been cumulative, with later studies building upon earlier results; this quality is reflected in Henderson and Beers (1980). These dissertations and their sequelae constitute the largest single body of work on creative spelling in school.

The first of these dissertations was by Beers (1974), who hypothesized a sequence of four spelling strategies for lax and tense vowels (/æ,ɛ,I,r,i,aI/) and then determined whether first and second graders in Charlottesville, Virginia (four classrooms at each grade) tended to move through this sequence during a period of six months. Beers's four stages are illustrated below for /ɛ/ in *step* (Beers, 1974, p. 32):

Strategy	Score	Example	Comment
omission of vowel	1	STP	least mature
letter-name	2	STAP	letter-name or tense/lax pairing
transitional	3	STAEP	standard correspondence or marker
correct form	4	STEP	standard spelling

Gentry (1977) modified this sequence and extended it to consonants. His five stages are illustrated below with spellings of *type* (Gentry, 1977, p. 23):

Strategy	Score	Example	Comment
Deviant	0	MENENA	Catchall; none of the other types
Prephonetic	1	TP	segment(s) omitted
Phonetic	2	TIP	letter-name or tense/lax pairing
Transitional	3	TIPE	standard correspondence or marker
Correct	4	TYPE	completely standard spelling

Gentry comments that children in the primary grades produce mainly spellings at the latter four stages; 'deviant' spellings are generally quite immature. Prephonetic spellings usually involve omissions without a phonetic basis, unlike those of preconsonantal nasals and vowels before syllabic sonorants. The transitional spellings 'usually satisfied one of three requirements:'

a) segment spelled incorrectly but with a possible standard spelling: MONSTOR for *monster*
b) reversals of standard spellings: TAOD for *toad*
c) segment spelled correctly but other parts of word non-standard: UNITTED for *united*. (p. 19)

Clearly, the main characteristic of transitional spellings for both Beers and Gentry is that they show the influence of standard spelling patterns without being standard. Gentry's third criterion, however, allows the spelling of one segment to influence the classification of other spellings in the same word. We cannot know how particular sounds were spelled, since the data are not presented in full.

Both Beers's and Gentry's results confirm that phonetic spellings like those seen in preschool do occur in the primary grades and that children progress through the hypothesized stages of spelling development. Both found greater variability and greater evidence of development among first graders than second graders; for the words used in these studies, second graders produced high proportions of transitional and standard spellings. Beers found that children progressed in the predicted direction for twenty-three of the twenty-four words presented. When children failed to progress, it was largely because of a ceiling effect: for some frequent words, they produced standard spellings early. Gentry observed an interaction of reading achievement and grade with spelling strategy. Table 2.1 is Gentry's summary of predominant spelling-types by grade and reading achievement (p. 87). Where phonetic spellings predominate, it is almost invariably among high-achievement kindergarteners and low- to middle-achievement first graders. Only for lax vowels do phonetic spellings fail to predominate at some point in this range.

In addition, Beers notes an apparent effect of frequency. He found more mature spellings for *light* and *ride* than for *tribe* and *dike*, for instance (p. 74). For some words, such as *lip*, it appeared that the relevant measure is frequency in children's reading materials, rather than the frequency reported in lists such as Thorndike and Lorge (1944).

TABLE 2.1 *Predominant spelling strategy used by nine achievement subgroups in spelling eight phonetic features from Gentry (1977)*

Subgroup	Phonetic Feature Category							
	Tense	Lax	Nasal	Sonorant	-ed	Retroflex	Affricates	Flap
K – low	D	D	D	D	D	D	D	D
K – middle	P	PP	PP	D	D	D	P	D
K – high	P	T	P	P	P	P	P	P
1 – low	P	PP	P	PP	PP	P	P	P
1 – middle	P	T	P	T	P	P	T	P
1 – high	T	T	C	T	P	T	T	P
2 – low	T	T	T	T	P	T	T	P
2 – middle	T	C	C	T	C	T	C	C
2 – high	C	C	C	T	C	C	C	C

Key: D = Deviant, PP = Prephonetic, P = Phonetic, T = Transitional, C = Correct.

Beers and Gentry have shown a general pattern of spelling development in kindergarten through the second grade, at least for words of one morpheme and in most cases, one syllable. A limitation of these studies is that the spelling strategies are rather vaguely defined. In particular, 'prephonetic' and 'transitional' both include some qualitatively different kinds of spelling. Gentry's definition of the latter, though more explicit than Beers's, makes it impossible for us to know how particular segments were represented.

D Marino

Marino (1978) assumed that although reading and spelling are not reciprocal, both draw upon knowledge of phonetic, graphemic and morphophonemic structure. Phonetic spellings, selected from Read (1975), were A for /ε/, omission of preconsonantal nasals, and CHR for /tr/. Graphemic patterns, based on Venezky (1970), included markers (such as final 'silent' *e* after a single consonant), positional rules (such as the occurrence of *u* after *q*), and doubling rules (such as *embed* + *-ed* yielding *embedded*). Morphophonemic spellings represented roots and their derived forms consistently despite differences in pronunciation, such as the *t* in *promote/promotion* and *suggest/suggestion*.

From 180 children in the second, third and fourth grades, Marino elicited spellings of these three types, dictating forty-five spelling words in sentence contexts, that is, fifteen words selected to elicit each type. Her principal hypothesis was that these levels increase in developmental complexity in the order named, so that overall, children would make most morphophonemic errors and fewest phonetic ones. In other words, she expected that the phonetic errors would decrease at the lower grade levels, followed by the graphemic and then the morphophonemic. She also expected that while morphophonemic errors would be most frequent and phonetic errors least frequent at each grade, the number of errors of each type would decrease with grade.

Except for the fact that graphemic errors did not become less frequent across the grades, the results essentially fit these predictions. The mean number of target errors at each linguistic level was significantly different from each other level (p. < .05) and there was a significant grade by level interaction (p. < .0001), with more phonetic errors at grade two than at grades three or four.

Marino selected the three phonetic spellings on the basis of a pilot study with first through fourth graders, in which these three spellings best predicted total performance. Because some stimulus words contained more than one of these patterns, the number of opportunities for each spelling was not equal: there were five /tr/'s but seven preconsonantal nasals and nine /ɛ/'s. Children did indeed produce the predicted spellings: at grade two, the three phonetic errors constituted 49.5 per cent of the total errors on 'target structures,' declining to 33 per cent at grade four. Overall, these phonetic errors ranked between the morphophonemic and the graphemic ones in the proportion of total errors accounted for. Marino concludes that the phonetic level is a real locus of spelling processes. She notes, however, that the 'use of phonetic representations beyond grade two was minimal' (pp. 82–3). In her pilot study, only a small number of children beyond grade one had produced the phonetic spellings, but those who did were consistent (p. 88), and even in grade four some children produced such spellings.

Marino also stratified her sample of children by performance on tests of reading and spelling, as 'good readers/good spellers,' 'good readers/poor spellers,' and 'poor readers/poor spellers.' Unfortunately, the proportions were very uneven across the three grades, with only a handful of good readers/poor spellers at grades two and three. This circumstance severely limited Marino's opportunity to draw inferences about performance by achievement. There was no significant difference in the frequency of phonetic errors across the three groups.

The graphemic errors are of interest precisely because they did not fit the predictions. They did not decline significantly across the grades, and while they were significantly less frequent than the morphophonemic errors at all grades, they were more frequent than phonetic spellings only at grades three and four. The poor readers/poor spellers did relatively well with the graphemic patterns, while making more morphophonemic errors than the other two groups (good readers). Marino conducted a supplementary study of fifth graders, to see whether these patterns persist. Again, the good readers made significantly fewer morphophonemic errors, but there was no difference across groups in number of graphemic errors (p. 67).

As Marino suggests (pp. 83-4), the unexpected results with graphemic errors may reflect the way in which that level was defined. It included various markers, conventions and constraints, such as capitalization, the occurrence of *-ck* only at the ends of morphemes, and the use of word-final *-e* after a single consonant to indicate length of a preceding vowel. These 'actually represent varying degrees of abstractness' (p. 83). In fact, the graphemic constraints do not correspond to a level of language at all, whereas the other two types have to do with representing phonemes vs. morphemes. As a result, graphemic constraints potentially overlap with the other two types. The way children learn a mixed bag of spelling conventions may well be different from the way they learn to represent constituents of their language. Marino suggests that for spelling research, Venezky's (1970) graphemic patterns should be subcategorized and refined.

Likewise, the morphological spellings could be subdivided. Inflectional vs. derivational morphemes, morphemes that affect the spelling of a root to which they are bound vs. those that do not, morphemes that affect pronunciation vs. those that do not – any of these dimensions may affect learning to spell. It would also be interesting to look for overgeneralization in spelling: DIVEED for *dived* is an overgeneralization in spelling in roughly the same sense that 'comed' for *came* is in young children's spoken language. Clearly, there is an opportunity for research that refines the categories with which Marino has begun.

This classificatory problem is really the same as the one that confronted Beers and Gentry, however. Especially beyond the preschool level, as children's spelling becomes subject to a wider variety of influences, most nonstandard spellings can be described in more than one way. In most cases, we do not yet know which descriptions correspond to spelling processes. We have more confidence in the phonetic basis for the spellings described in Chapter 1 partly because there are few plausible competing explanations in most cases, and partly because experiments suggest that the phonetic explanations are tenable. However, as is so often the case in psychology, spelling behavior itself does not indicate what the processes must be.

Even where we have plausible theories of spelling processes, we still need studies of how they interact. Marino showed that both phonetic and morphophonemic errors occur, and with different developmental histories. Her study was not designed to show that there are distinct phonetic and morphological spelling strategies, nor what happens when these putative strategies are both applicable (in what order?) or when they conflict.

E Treiman

Treiman (1982) studied children's (and adults') spelling and pronunciation of stops after initial /s/, as in *spy*, *sty* and *sky*. Although these stops are spelled as the voiceless /p/, /t/ and /k/, they are actually like the voiced counterparts /b/, /d/ and /g/ in both voice onset time and lack of aspiration. Thus children who are not yet influenced by standard spelling should classify these stops as /b/, /d/ and /g/.

This is precisely what Treiman observed: although most children in her sample spelled these clusters *sp-*, *st-* and *sk-* in nonce stimuli, a minority spelled them *sb-*, *sd-* and *sg-*. These children were at lower (first- and second-grade) reading levels, and thus less familiar with standard spelling. However, they were no less consistent than those who produced standard spellings, no less accurate on control items, and no less competent on a pretest of spelling stops initially, where the voiceless ones contrast with the voiced ones in both voicing and aspiration. By contrast, Treiman found (as have phonetics teachers) that adults are so influenced by standard spelling that only with difficulty can they become aware that the stop in *spy* is more like that in *buy* than that in *pie*. This study therefore supports the hypothesis that children's spelling at first reflects phonetic judgments, and only later do the judgments suggested by standard spelling become dominant.

Treiman has also analyzed more than 5600 spellings by forty-three first graders. Preliminary results reveal many of the phonetic spellings described in Chapter 1 and some new ones. For instance, Treiman (1983) confirms the nonstandard spellings of flaps (EDR for *eater*), the use of CHR for /tr/ and JR for /dr/ (CHRAP for *trap*), the use of R for /ɚ/ and L for syllabic /l/ (BRUTR for *brother* and LITL for *little*), phonetically-accurate spellings of the three pronunciations of the past tense morpheme (LIKT for *liked*, CAD for *called*, and SQRDID for *squirted*), and the rarity of Z for the /z/ and /əz/ pronunciations of plural, possessive and third-person verb suffixes.

Among new observations, she reports the use of a consonant letter to spell its own name (BAB for *baby*), and the use of T and D to represent the affricates /č/ and /ǰ/ (TESE for *cheese* and DAM for *jam*). (These affricates really begin with [t] and [d], being phonetically [tš] and [dž] respectively.) She also notes (Treiman, in press) the frequent omission of the second consonant in a syllable-initial consonant cluster (SRRS for *stars* and BUDRFI for *butterfly*).

In this corpus of spellings, Treiman is examining omissions in consonant clusters in general, i.e., omissions of obstruents, liquids and nasals in both initial and final clusters, taking into account the effects of frequency and letter-names. She suggests (personal communication, 1983) that such omissions may be dependent on syllable structure. For example, second consonants in initial clusters and first consonants in final clusters are vulnerable, regardless of sound type. Such a unified account of omissions in relation to syllable structure is appealing. It is not necessarily incompatible with Read's (1975) explanation of the omission of preconsonantal nasals in terms of phonetic properties, which can account for the influence of preceding vowels (which Treiman has not found in her data) and of following voiceless consonants, both of which affect the duration of preconsonantal nasals, and for possible differences in the frequency of omission of obstruents, liquids and nasals. Both syllable structure and phonetic form may play a role in a complete account; Chapter 4 presents additional evidence from other languages.

Thus there are both similarities and differences between Read's (1975) and Treiman's (1983) data, collected at different ages, in different dialect areas, and under somewhat different circumstances. Even more important, there are questions of how best to explain similar data and of how multiple influences interact. Raising and eventually answering such questions shows how spelling can be used to test hypotheses about the development of literacy.

III Conclusion

The studies reviewed in this chapter have shown quite clearly that the patterns previously observed in the preschool (Chapter 1) also occur in the primary grades. Not all patterns have been shown in every study, and the frequencies have varied somewhat. For instance, A for /ɛ/ ranged from at least 33 per cent in Gates to 17 per cent in Gerritz. Still, the most frequent tense-lax pairings (A for /ɛ/ and E for /I/), the omission of preconsonantal nasals, the omission of vowel spellings before final sonorants, and even CHR for /tr/ have been seen in the spelling of first and second graders. In addition, Beers, Gentry and Marino have at least outlined the development in spelling during the primary grades. While some of the categories are predictable (that prephonetic spellings come first and standard spellings last), and others are rather vaguely defined ('transitional'), this work nevertheless provides a general picture of the way in which beginning spelling develops from a phonetic basis toward more varied and abstract bases, and therefore toward standard spelling.

3 Dialects and spelling

The preceding chapters show that when young children spell, they rely heavily on their phonetic judgments. This naturally leads to the question of whether their spelling depends on their pronunciation, and therefore on their dialect. In fact, earlier theories of teaching spelling held that spelling errors arise from 'mispronunciations,' whether articulatory, dialectal or nonsystematic. Thus it was thought that if all school children could be taught the 'proper' pronunciation of words, there would be far fewer spelling problems. (See Wolff (1952) for an example of this approach, and Groff (1973) for a summary and critique of such views.) The question addressed in this chapter is whether dialect differences in pronunciation have any appreciable effect on spelling performance.

What one would hope for in research on this topic is a range of material from preschoolers through approximately grade two, where reliance on phonetic strategies in spelling diminishes. Unfortunately, the field has not been so well covered, and the studies available do not include any children at the ages at which phonetic strategies are most salient. Thus in this chapter we present a number of studies of older children from which we must make inferences about invented spellings by young children.

I The concept of dialect

An implicit assumption of many dialect studies is that dialects are deviations from a norm, especially from so-called Standard English (SE). In fact there is no Standard English dialect; there are only standards of pronunciation and usage set by the prescriptive grammar which plays so large a part in our educational experience, or by the speech style of the broadcast media. Everyone is a speaker of some dialect(s), but no one of them is standard English. SE might more accurately be characterized as a style or register of English, namely that used by educated speakers in relatively formal speaking and writing. The association with education, formality and (indirectly) social class gives rise to the belief that SE is a basic, normative dialect, from which a multitude of inferior dialects diverge.

The linguistic criterion of mutual intelligibility for dialects is often confounded with political and geographical boundaries as well as with prestige. For example, Danish and Norwegian are so closely related as to be dialects of the same language, yet the political borders lead us to call them separate languages. In contrast, Cantonese and Mandarin are called dialects of Chinese but in fact are mutually unintelligible, differing even in tonal systems.

Returning to the concept of style, it has been found (Labov, 1972; Wolfram and Fasold, 1974) that most native speakers vary their style according to the demands of the communicative situation. It is not the case that at one end of the spectrum is 'dialectal' speech and at the other 'standard,' but rather a range of style exists within each person's dialect or ideolect. Researchers must beware of this ability to switch styles, because a certain style in the presence of an interviewer or in a test situation does not mean that the speaker uses that style exclusively or even ordinarily. However, young children have less versatility in style than adults. Exposure to written materials and practice in reading and writing may strengthen the ability to switch styles. Growing awareness, with age, of prejudices toward particular dialect features may also contribute to the motivation to use more formal styles fluently.

In the literature 'dialect' is sometimes used almost interchangeably with 'class' or 'race.' Dialect should be defined by linguistic criteria, but it is inevitably confounded with political, sociocultural and economic factors. Thus, in the studies we will be reviewing, dialect is not and cannot be one-dimensionally defined.

Another assumption implicit in many dialect and spelling studies is that standard spelling reflects Standard English. Actually, standard spelling probably reflects no one dialect more directly than any other. A speaker of 'received pronunciation,' a prestige dialect of Great Britain, might pronounce *where* as [hwɛə] and *wear* [wɛə], while a speaker of educated Midwestern American English, which is close to a broadcast standard in the United States, might pronounce both words [wɛɚ]. Standard spelling reflects the British speaker's distinction between [hw] and [w], but it fails to match his 'r-less' pronunciation of the final sound, while for the Midwestern American, the situation is reversed. For every dialect, some features of pronunciation are directly represented in the orthography, while others are not. Standard spelling could not represent all dialects and, in fact, it does not represent any dialect directly, not even a prestigious one.

A Relevance of dialect-spelling studies to linguistic theory

If English orthography represents abstract lexical forms, as Chomsky and Halle (1968) argue, studies of spelling errors may show the extent to which these lexical forms are available to the speaker of a language, i.e., how 'psychologically real' they are. Beginning spellers rely on their phonetic and phonological knowlege, but in order to produce consistent or standard spelling, they must gradually learn to draw on knowledge at a more abstract level. (Acquiring lexical structures is probably accelerated by exposure to written materials; becoming a proficient speller and reader may aid a child's linguistic development as much as the linguistic development aids his spelling and reading proficiency.) Asking a child in an early stage to spell words which are unfamiliar in their written form may force him or her to use this deeper knowledge.

Comparing spelling errors across dialects may shed light on the question of how abstract the lexical (underlying) forms of words are. If speakers of all dialects rely on similar lexical representations, then spelling errors should not differ significantly across dialects. Conversely, if speakers of distinct dialects differ in the types of errors that they make, then either spellers do not rely on abstract lexical representations or the lexical form is not uniform across dialects. The latter would argue for less abstract deep structures in phonological description.

II Dialect studies

Dialects can be divided into social and regional varieties. Regional dialects are defined geographically; social dialects are defined by socioeconomic and sociocultural characteristics. Black English is the best-known example of an American social dialect, and we will begin our review with a discussion of several studies of Black English (BE), followed by one of Chicano English. We will then discuss the possible influences of socioeconomic class on spelling performance. Finally, we will discuss the evidence for effects of regional dialect on spelling.

A Social dialects

1 Black English

Most of the research on spelling and social dialect has been done on Black English. In the early 1970s, Kligman and Cronnell carried out a series of studies of the comparative effects of Black English and Standard English on spelling (Kligman and Cronnell, 1974; Kligman, Cronnell and Verna, 1972). Their topic was not direct effects of BE phonology on spelling patterns but rather indirect effects on overall spelling proficiency. Their studies were conducted on second graders in Los Angeles, in both predominantly black and predominantly white schools. They gave a multiple-choice spelling test which contained words with forty-three phonological features in which BE differs from SE, as well as several control features shared by both dialects.

The BE speakers made significantly more errors than SE speakers (43 per cent vs. 36 per cent). For both groups combined there were more non-dialect related errors (23 per cent) than dialect (BE) related errors (16 per cent), and the rate of non-dialect errors was nearly the same for both groups, leading the researchers to conclude that general spelling performance does not differ by dialect (Kligman *et al.*, 1972, p. 1250).

The dialect-related errors were of six types. (The terminology may be confusing; both SE and BE speakers made dialect-related errors, but the dialect referred to is always BE.)

   1   /ɛ/ before nasals is pronounced /I/ in BE. Thus *pen* is

pronounced /pIn/ and may be spelled PIN. This is said to be a strong BE trait, but also a growing southern Californian one; for both groups the error rate was greater than 50 per cent.

2   /sks/ or /sts/ at the end of a plural noun or the third person singular verb reduces to /sk/ or /st/. Thus *desks* is pronounced /desk/ and spelled DESK. Two-thirds of the BE-speaking children made this error, and one-half of the SE-speakers did. The authors suggest that this is a developmental error rather than a dialectal BE one.

3   The /t/ or /d/ forms of the past tense (*helped, raised*) are omitted by two-thirds of the BE-speakers and by one-half of the SE-speakers. For both groups this form was more often misspelled than the /əd/ form of the past tense (*wanted*).

4   The /əz/ form of the plural (*churches*) is commonly deleted by both groups. The authors attribute this error to child language development, like type (2), stating that the /s/ and /z/ forms (*cups, cubs*) are usually mastered earlier than the /əz/ form.

5   /ɛ/ before non-nasal consonants is pronounced /I/ in BE. For example, *wet* is pronounced /wIt/ and may be spelled WIT. This spelling was more frequent from the SE speakers (50 per cent) than for the BE speakers (25 per cent). The authors attribute this to the growing merger of /ɛ/ and /I/ in southern Californian speech.

6   Medial /l/ is deleted in BE speech. For example *bulb* may be pronounced /bəb/ and spelled BUB. Fifty per cent of BE speakers produced the corresponding spelling, versus 25 per cent of SE speakers (1972, p. 1251f).

There were non-significant effects of such BE features as deletion in contractions, deletion of plural markers and possessive markers, changing of final /θ/ to /f/, and others. In addition, some features of BE were completely unrelated to spelling errors, such as the deletion of /r/ in initial clusters (Kligman *et al.*, 1972, p. 1252).

The features of BE which were the easiest and the most difficult were the same for both groups, but on the whole BE speakers made more errors on these than did SE speakers. From easiest to most difficult, these features were (Kligman and Cronnell, 1974, p. 48):

for BE speakers	*for SE speakers*
word-final *d*	word-final *d*
word-final *s*	word-final *th*
'*s* (contraction	'*s* (contraction
and possessive)	and possessive)
word-final *th*	word-final *s*
medial *l*	medial *l*
-*ed* (past tense)	-*ed* (past tense)

The authors state (1974, p. 22) that this similarity between the groups is 'not surprising.' They give three possible reasons: 1 BE and the dialect(s) of low-income whites are similar; 2 BE-related errors may in fact be 'related to the nature of English'; 3 some features of BE are similar to features of child language development, which is still going on in the second grade. Yet the BE features chosen for study were some of those which define BE. Contrary to the reasonable expectation that BE features would be reflected in the spelling of BE speakers, Kligman and Cronnell found that the expected errors are frequent in both groups. What is not clear is the extent to which these errors actually correspond to SE, as well as BE, pronunciation, as is apparently the case for errors 1 (PIN for *pen*) and 5 (WIT for *wet*). At any rate, the most frequent errors appear not to be morphological or graphemic and may be phonetic for both groups.

There were three features which BE-speaking children spelled correctly more often than SE speakers:

1 /ɛ/ before non-nasals; the so-called BE-related errors on this feature were twice as frequent for SE speakers. Some creative spellers also produced this spelling at a late stage, revising the earlier use of E for /I/ (Read, 1975, p. 40).
2 -*ing* as in *reading*, pronounced [In] in BE but (sometimes) [Iŋ] in SE.
3 /ɛ/ before *r*, as in *bear*. BE speech tends to raise /ɛ/ so that *bear* and *beer* are homophonous. Yet BE children produced correct spellings more often than SE children, and they chose the BE-related error type *BEER* less often than the SE group. Again, the explanation is not clear. The children had to choose from three alternative spellings: BEAR, BEER or BAR. Like the creative spellers (Chapter 1), they might use A for /ɛ/, and in fact they did

choose BAR more often than BE children did, but the difference was not statistically significant. BE children applying the same strategy would likely produce BER, but the choices were BEER and BEAR, which are perhaps equally attractive from this point of view.

It is unfortunate that the test format was multiple choice so that the children were not free to produce their own spellings. Many of the sets of choices did not include a phonetic spelling (in the sense of Chapter 1) of a BE pronunciation.

Sullivan (1971) compared the spelling of white and black second graders in San Antonio and Austin. In general, the results are consistent with those of Kligman and Cronnell in that black children had more difficulty with standard orthography than white children did. However, there are flaws in the research design which may have affected the outcomes. The white students were from predominantly suburban, affluent families, while the black students were from poor, urban families (Groff, 1973). Nor did Sullivan attempt to control variables like reading ability and measured intelligence, which are also correlated with social class.

O'Neal and Trabasso (1976) also studied the relation between spelling and pronunciation for BE and SE speakers. They tested third and fifth graders on 128 words from Labov's (1967) lists of Black English pronunciations. They assumed that younger children would make more unconventional spellings and rely more on phonetic information than the older ones.

O'Neal and Trabasso contrasted black/white with urban/suburban dialect features; their sample included black and white inner city students and white suburban students. There were four classes of words, with sixteen pairs in each:

 — 'Lect Neutral' (pairs which are not homophonous in either dialect, e.g., *away/tray*;
 — 'Standard English Confusable' pairs which may be homophonous in SE, e.g., *are/or*;
 — 'Black English Confusable' pairs which may be homophonous in BE, e.g., *ball/boil*;
 — 'Black English Changes or Deletions,' words which often undergo some phonological change in BE, e.g., *booth*: /bu/, /buf/, /but/ (p. 174).

To half of the students the words were given in isolation, to see if they are perceived as homophonous without a disambiguating context. To the other half they were given with an example sentence. The researchers expected the SE speakers to make SE mistakes and the BE speakers to make BE mistakes.

O'Neal and Trabasso conclude that dialect differences in pronunciation do affect spelling (p. 185). Black children did not actually confuse BE-confusable words more often than white children did, but with overall spelling ability controlled, black children created more unconventional spellings for BE Confusable and BE Change/Deletion words than did the white children especially in third grade.

The unconventional spellings were found to be correlated with the phonology of BE. The black third graders made a higher percentage of predicted spellings for final /θ/, substitution of /I/ for /ɛ/ before nasals, and for several final consonants and consonant clusters, compared to urban white third graders. Black fifth graders made none of these errors except for final /t/ (p. 184).

Interestingly, O'Neal and Trabasso also found that the urban blacks and whites shared some 'phonological' spellings: consonant cluster reductions and medial *th* → *d*. In addition, urban white children made more *E* → *I* before nasals, plural /s/ deletions, and final /d/ deletions than did suburban whites. They infer that there must be some similarities between black and white urban dialects (p. 184f).

In attempting to consider factors other than phonology, the authors note that the BE words were longer and less frequent than the dialect-neutral or SE confusable words. They caution that this may have been the reason for the larger number of unconventional spellings (p. 187).

O'Neal and Trabasso conclude that perhaps phonology plays a larger role in the spelling of words unfamiliar in their written form than in familiar ones. Not surprisingly, meaning plays a large part in reducing reliance on phonetic information; the reduction in perceived homophony in sentence contexts was 50 per cent across all of the groups in both grades (p. 180). The incidence of unconventional spellings decreases with age, for all students.

O'Neal and Trabasso's (rather obvious) suggestion that the written familiarity of a word is important is supported by Farnham-Diggory (1978). She found that black children (assumed to be speakers of BE) seem to prefer a visual strategy while white children (assumed to be speakers of SE) prefer a sound strategy. That is, black children in her study took less time to spell when words were presented to them visually rather than in dictation; the opposite was true for the white children. Farnham-Diggory suggests that the BE speakers were 'attempting to recode the sounds of words into visual form when spelling from dictation.' She attributes this strategy to dialect differences, suggesting that if a child is aware that his/her teacher pronounces words differently, i.e., is a speaker of SE, and the child is a BE speaker, the child 'might be well-advised to try to remember what it looks like in order to spell it,' because relying on one's own pronunciation will result in misspelling. Farnham-Diggory cites evidence that black children produce more correct letters – 'visual frames' – in misspelled words than white children do (p. 79f).

Cronnell (1982a) examined writing produced by inner-city, low-income black children in the third and sixth grades in Los Angeles to determine the possible influences of Black English on their writing. The errors produced were classified as 'possible BE influence,' 'possible hypercorrection from BE' and 'no obvious BE influence or hypercorrection' (p. 3).

Thirty-nine per cent of the third graders' mistakes were attributed to possible BE influence, and 33 per cent of the sixth graders'. These errors included grammatical and morphological as well as spelling mistakes. The classification of errors is potentially misleading because the categories 'verbs' and 'nouns' include mistakes which might as easily be due to pronunciation-to-spelling correspondences as to grammatical influences. For example, third person singular -*s* on verbs was omitted by 15 per cent of the third graders and 10 per cent of the sixth graders. Likewise, plural and possessive -*s* were omitted by 11 per cent of the third graders and 8 per cent of the sixth graders (pp. 6-9).

There were two phonological categories, 'consonants' and 'vowels.' The major error with consonants was final consonant-cluster reductions, e.g., PON for *pond*. Less frequently, single final consonants were omitted, e.g., MOTHE for *mother*, *th* was spelled T or D a few times, and *wh* was sometimes spelled W. Consonantal mistakes totaled 27 per cent and 29 per cent for third and sixth graders respectively. Of these 9 per cent and 13 per cent were final consonant clusters (pp. 6-9).

Cronnell writes that vowel misspellings can be attributed to dialectal influence with much less certainty, since English vowels are so problematic for all children in general. They accounted for 6 per cent and 5 per cent for third and sixth graders respectively. The only possibly BE-influenced vowel misspelling that Cronnell mentions is the substitution of I for E before nasals, e.g., THIN for *then*. Even here he cautions that raising occurs in many dialects of English, especially in southern California (p. 9).

Cronnell concludes that there are some dialect influences in the writing of Black English speakers, but that dialect is not the predominant source of errors for these children.

2 Chicano English

Cronnell (1982b) did a preliminary study of linguistic effects in the writings of third- and sixth-grade Chicano children from low-income families in urban Los Angeles. The study included grammatical variations as well as spelling, but we will review only the latter.

Cronnell notes that Chicano English is by no means a uniform dialect; both English and Spanish are possible influences, since some Chicanos are monolingual English or Spanish speakers, and some are bilingual. In any case, Spanish is assumed to have at least an indirect effect on the English of Chicanos. Cronnell does not describe the language spoken by the children studied, but attempts to discern possible interlanguage influences on their writing (p. 1f).

Thirty-three per cent of the errors in the third graders' compositions could be attributed to possible language influence, and 36 per cent of those in the sixth graders' (p. 5f). The third graders' errors more often included spelling errors, while the sixth graders' were more in syntax and vocabulary (p. 6).

What Cronnell calls 'Spanish spellings' are those employing Spanish rather than English sound-to-spelling correspondences. For example, /i/ is spelled I (4 per cent occurrence), /a/ is spelled A (3 per cent), and /e/ is spelled E (2 per cent) among the third graders. The percentages for sixth graders were 2 per cent, 1 per cent and 0.5 per cent respectively. Examples of these 'Spanish spellings' are CLIN for *clean*, RACK for *rock* and MEKIN for *making* (p. 6f).

Another category contains spellings that appear to reflect

Spanish pronunciation, even when used by monolingual English speakers. The most frequent error of this type is reduction of final consonant clusters, e.g., HAN for *hand* (p. 10). Other examples of Spanish-influenced pronunciations reflected in spelling include substitution of /d/ for /θ/ (D for TH), /č/ for /š/ (CH for SH) and /s/ for /z/ (S for Z). There were also a few B/V confusions and some final consonant omissions (p. 10f).

Vowel pronunciations include /æ/ for /ɛ/ before /l/ (TALL for *tell*) and the frequent substitution of /a/ for English /ə/, spelled A or O (OP for *up*, FAN for *fun*) and /ar/ for /ɚ/ (SHART for *shirt*). Although Spanish does not have /I/ and speakers usually substitute /i/, there were almost no English /i/ spellings, i.e., EE for EA (p. 10ff). Cronnell offers no explanation, but we note that the standard Spanish spelling for /i/ (I) is the standard English spelling for /I/ (*fit*), so that Spanish-influenced pronunciation and spelling would yield standard English spelling. A Chicano learner would write *fit* precisely because he pronounced it 'feet.'

Cronnell's preliminary study is encouraging for further research in the rich area of Chicano English. Certainly one of the next steps should be to describe adequately the phonology of the several varieties of Chicano English. The data presented by Cronnell contain definite phonetic influences. Studies of even younger children should prove to be of great interest as well.

3 Social class

Stever's (1976) dissertation is concerned with separating the influences of social class and dialect on spelling. She adopts Beers's (1974) hierarchy of spelling strategies, and hypothesizes that dialect (pronunciation) would not influence the spelling proficiency of second graders, but socio-economic status would adversely affect a child's progression through the Beers hierarchy.

Children from three Alexandria, Virginia schools were given one spelling test per month for five months. The children were socioeconomically stratified according to their parents' occupations, and if any of their pronunciations differed from SE, they were classified as speakers of Variant English (Southern American English).

Socioeconomic class did not significantly affect spelling, although the lower-class children made slightly more errors. Dialect (pronunciation) was found not to hinder progression through the hierarchy of strategies. At any given level of development, the same strategy applies, regardless of the child's dialect. These strategies sometimes yield nonstandard spellings like those described in Chapter 1, such as E for /I/ and A for /ɛ/. Stever suspects that since most children in second grade are beyond these vowel-pairing strategies, the children in her sample may have been too advanced for her to make accurate distinctions among the effects of spelling strategies, social class and dialect.

B Regional dialects

1 Graham and Rudorf

Graham and Rudorf (1970) conducted a study of regional dialects to test the hypothesis that spelling errors would be uniform across dialects. They were testing the general applicability of the results of a study done at Stanford (Hanna, Hanna, Hodges and Rudorf, 1966) which found that for Standard English, as represented by Merriam-Webster's *New International Dictionary*, Second Edition, there is a predictable pattern of phoneme-grapheme correspondence. Hanna *et al.* found that a computer could spell about 50 per cent of 17,000 words correctly on the basis of sound cues alone (Graham and Rudorf, 1970, p. 364).

Three dialect areas were selected. The Western Reserve area of Ohio was chosen as most nearly representing the pronunciations which had been taken to be standard in the Stanford study. To this they compared the dialects of the Boston area and the rural environs of Atlanta. Graham and Rudorf compared the proportions of phoneme-errors with word-errors in the spellings of the dialect groups and concluded that the significant differences in these proportions are attributable to the influence of dialect on spelling, i.e., that the conclusions of the Stanford study do not hold up when other dialects are considered. They further conclude that a child must use phonological cues in spelling unfamiliar words and that the 'standard code of phoneme-grapheme correspondences is less applicable to the speech of the inhabitants of Zebulon, Georgia than it is to the speakers of the other dialects studied' (p. 374), that is, that standard spelling represents some dialects better than others.

What we can glean from this study is that older children too use phonetic cues in spelling, and to that extent, dialect does play a part. But it must also be borne in mind that by the time they reach the sixth grade, children have more knowledge of the deeper phonological, morphological and orthographic levels, and so have more varied representations on which to base their spelling. Graham and Rudorf consider word familiarity but not these other (non-phonetic) levels of representation. They apparently discount the sixth graders' experience in reading and writing, which would promote a more abstract representation. Dialects clearly differ more in pronunciation than in abstract lexical representation, if they differ in the latter at all. If dialect is responsible in part for some spelling difficulties of sixth graders, then it should have a stronger effect on the spelling of younger, less linguistically sophisticated children.

2 Appalachia

The Appalachian community is, geographically and socially, relatively isolated from the rest of the United States, and the dialect of the area is correspondingly distinct. This situation could be ideal for the study of dialect and spelling, but so far it has been neglected, except for one study conducted by Boiarsky (1969).

Boiarsky studied Appalachian tenth graders, who are older than the children of interest to us, but the results are revealing nonetheless. The students were matched with a group of tenth graders from Philadelphia, who had similar socioeconomic backgrounds and IQ levels. The Philadelphia students represented a 'standard dialect,' and the spelling test administered concentrated on the differences between the two. For instance, SE /ε/ corresponds to /e/ or /i/ in Appalachian; SE /i/ to /I/ or /ε/; and SE /e/ to /ε/ or /I/.

The results of the spelling tests were as follows. On all but one word (*wreck*) the Appalachian students made far more errors in spelling than did the Philadelphia students, and a very large percentage of the errors could be attributed to the dialect differences. For example, Appalachian *fell* is pronounced /fel/ or /fil/; the spelling errors include FAIL, FEIL and FEEL. All of these spellings represent reasonable spellings of the dialect pronunciations, and they account for almost all of the misspellings. Boiarsky does not give any examples of non-dialect-related errors, so no inferences can be made about those.

There seems to be no regular correlation between pronunciation and number of errors made. Words like *well* and *hill* were pronounced by a great percentage of the students (77 per cent and 61 per cent respectively) as /wil/ or /wel/ and /hil/, yet very few dialect-related errors were made on these words. Eighty per cent of the Appalachian students pronounced *fill* as /fil/ but only 4 per cent misspelled it accordingly. Boiarsky conjectures that the reasons for these pronunciation 'deviations' are the phonetic environments, i.e., that the initial *st* cluster explains the raising of the vowel in *still*. There appears to be no phonetic basis for this assertion, but there may be for her other speculation, that the final /l/ in words such as *fill* explains the raising of the vowel. Raising does occur frequently in just those words that end in /l/: four out of six of the stimulus words with /i/ for SE /I/ end in /l/ and all have the high vowel 60 per cent of the time or more. This might be due to the 'darkness' (velarization) of syllable-final /l/ in English, which colors the vowel as well. All but one of the words representing the reverse change – /i/ becoming /I/ or /ɛ/ – also end in /l/, but the frequencies of this change are much lower (23 per cent for one, 1 per cent to 6 per cent for the rest). Fully two-thirds of the monosyllabic stimulus words ended in /l/ (there were just two polysyllabic words) (p. 348f). It would be interesting to know if these vowel shifts occur almost exclusively in this environment, as the word lists suggest, or if the choice of stimuli is accidental.

The Appalachian dialect as described by Boiarsky is characterized by changes in vowel height as compared with SE, and the number of related spelling errors is so much greater than for the Philadelphia students that she concludes that there must be a relationship between dialect and spelling. Her study suggests that this is potentially a fruitful area for further study of dialect and spelling, particularly among younger children.

3 Virginia

A wealth of data on spelling acquisition of children in Virginia is available, but most of the studies do not take into account the possible effects of dialect on spelling, despite indications that there is such an effect. The dialect in Virginia is usually labelled general Southern, although there are several subdialects. Studies show that general Southern dialect is distinct from standard American English at the phonemic as well as the allophonic level (Kurath and McDavid, 1961).

One is tempted to reexamine the results of the Virginia studies for the effects of dialect, but the data given in the final reports of the studies are usually not detailed enough for reinterpretation. Such an attempt would be of questionable value anyway, since the subjects were not selected according to shared (sub)dialect, native dialect, or level of linguistic development. A few hints of the effects of dialect can be gleaned, however.

Zutell (1975) found a high proportion of first and second graders in Culpeper, Virginia, who omitted the inflectional ending -*ed* in their writings. He suggests that this may be due to dialect: 'southern speech in general, and rural Virginia dialect in particular' tend to drop inflectional endings. The spelling TRIM for *trimmed* is phonetically accurate for these children. This is one plausible explanation. In reviewing the Black English studies, we mentioned that children seem to acquire morphophonemic knowledge rather late. If so, this fact of linguistic development would also help explain the omission of -*ed*. In fact, phonetically unrealized inflectional endings may delay the acquisition of morphemic knowledge.

III Conclusions

The studies in this chapter all support the idea that dialect does have some influence on spelling performance; some nonstandard spellings reflect actual pronunciation. While it seems certain that spelling strategies are correlated with stages of linguistic development, none of the studies reported here permits us to formulate predictions about what effects dialect might have on spelling strategies. This is in part due to the difficulty in avoiding false inferences; it is too easy to attribute tendencies in children's spelling to influence from dialect rather than to general linguistic development. Moreover, it is a mistake to assume that the phonetic strategies operate alone at any level of spelling development. While phonetic input is primary in the earlier years, a child later acquires a repertoire of strategies based on morphology and graphemic conventions; these strategies then play a greater role in spelling.

Studies discussed in Chapter 1 and 2 have shown that phonetic (invented) spellings occur in children from regions as diverse as New England, the Midwest and the South. They also come from a wide variety of socioeconomic backgrounds, from lower-class through upper-middle-class. By and large, these studies have identified the same invented spellings across these varied regions and social classes. Thus we appear to be in the anomalous position of arguing that the invented spellings have a phonetic basis and yet claiming that they are not affected by differences in pronunciation. The resolution is that the spellings that have been most widely observed – the vowel pairings, the omission of preconsonantal nasals, and the representation of syllabic sonorants with a single letter – derive from phonetic properties that are relatively unaffected by dialect variation. While vowels differ across dialects, the relationships between 'long' and 'short' vowels that are similar in place of articulation tends to remain. That is, while /ɛ/ may be raised, lowered, diphthongized, lengthened or nasalized in various geographical or social context, the letter-name vowel that it is closest to is still likely to be /e/. Certainly Malecot (1960) showed that nasals are short in the preconsonantal position across a variety of American dialects. Similarly, /l/, /m/ and /n/ tend to be syllabic when they follow obstruents, regardless of dialect. Thus the main invented spellings may be phonetic and yet stable across dialects.

Studies of dialect influences on children's spelling have revealed some effects of pronunciation on spelling, but not large or consistent ones. However, with the benefit of hindsight we can see several defects in these studies. In most cases they have dealt with children in the upper elementary grades, where we would expect less reliance on pronunciation and greater effects of reading experience and knowledge of relationships among words. These factors are correlated with social class; in this way dialect influences have been confounded in some studies with differences in social and educational background.

In addition, some of the studies have suffered from faulty notions of dialect and of the relationship between spelling and pronunciation, resulting sometimes in indenfensible conclusions. As a group, they have not built upon a coherent view of spelling development and the mechanisms by which dialect might influence spelling, nor have they observed changes with age or taken account of sufficient phonetic detail.

Despite these limitations, the studies are consistent with our general picture of spelling development; amidst all the other influences, there is indeed an effect of pronunciation on spelling, especially for younger children.

4 Beginning spelling in other languages

I Why study other languages?

The preceding chapters demonstrate that we can learn a great deal from analyses of children's beginning spelling in English, but there are severe limitations on what we can learn from any one language. Letter-names constitute one such limitation; other languages typically use other names for letters and so present young children with different spelling choices from those in English. In the United States, Canada and Great Britain, letter-names receive much attention in preschools and in books, television programs and now computer programs for preschoolers. Children in these cultures often begin with the assumption that the letter-names are guides to spelling, writing DA for *day* and FEL for *feel*, for example. Yet it would be interesting to know what spellings children might devise for these speech sounds if they did not correspond to letter-names. For example, would children ever represent /i/ with, say, U, relating it to another high vowel (/u/)?

Second, the structure of English words affects what we will learn from young children's spelling. In English, children must eventually learn morphological spellings, i.e., consistent spellings for parts of words that are related in meaning, like *wid-* in *wide* and *width* or *telegraph-* in *telegraphy* and *telegraphic*, despite the fact that the vowels in these pairs of words are pronounced differently. Do children more readily learn the *u* spelling in *reduction* (cf. *reduce*) than in *pronunciation* (cf. *pronounce*)? The spelling of the former pair is morphologically predictable, whereas that of the latter pair is phonologically predictable; which basis do young children find more natural, at what stage? We cannot fully answer such questions on the basis of English alone, since the words involved are not familiar to young children. Most of the morphologically-related sets of words spelled consistently in English are like *telegraphy* rather than *width*: learned, polysyllabic and technical words derived from Latin or Greek. Children are not likely to write these words, and if we ask them to do so, they may not know the relationships in meaning. A language with phonological alternations like *telegraphy/telegraphic*, but among more familiar words, would help us to see whether (or at what stage) children try to represent meaning relationships in their spelling.

A third restriction on the evidence that we can get from English alone is the non-occurrence or infrequency of various types of speech sounds. We mentioned in Chapter 1 that children tend to create similar spellings for all vowels that are back and rounded. Since these two qualities generally go together in English, we cannot tell which of them more strongly influences children's spelling. Given a choice, would children treat back rounded vowels as more like other rounded vowels or other back vowels? Front rounded vowels do occur in many other languages, making such a choice possible. Similarly, certain phonemes that do occur in English are rare and of limited distribution. /ž/ is such a case: it never occurs at the beginnings of syllables in native English words and is rare in any other position. It also tends to occur in rather learned words like *illusion*. As a result, in the data of Read (1975), this phoneme was spelled exactly once (as SH in YOUSHAWALL for *usual*), whereas most other phonemes were represented hundreds of times. Yet because /ž/ is one member of four pairs of fricatives in English, it would be interesting to know how children represent it with respect to the others; is it really closer to /š/ than to /z/, as the one spelling suggests?

Observing children's beginning spelling in other languages can help us to answer questions like these because other languages typically have systems of speech sounds that are different from that of English. In fact, it is almost never the case that two languages have the same phonemic systems, although certain systems of vowels and, less commonly, consonants, do appear in more than one language. Typically, a language may have *some* of the same vowel-types and *some* of the same consonant-types as English, but in different relationships. In 1925, Sapir pointed out that one language's /s/ may be functionally like another language's /š/ with respect to its place within a system. Since perceived similarities among speech sounds affect children's beginning spelling, we can learn much more about such judgments by studying how they vary across languages.

We must also test our theories about the beginnings of literacy against languages with a non-alphabetic writing system, such as Japanese or Chinese. For instance, it has been suggested that the hardest problem for some children in learning to read and write alphabetically is the difficulty of isolating individual phonemes (Liberman, Shankweiler, Liberman, Fowler and Fischer, 1977). One reason that segmentation is difficult is that, in normal pronunciation, adjacent phonemes influence one another so extensively that isolating any one of them is artificial. In *dog* (or any other word), what we think of as the individual segments [dɔg] is really a single continuous stream of sound with some characteristics of [d] or [g] occurring in the middle of the stream. In writing, we impose a segmentation which is not a physical reality.

The effect of segmentation difficulty on beginning reading and spelling can be tested by studying children's progress in languages with syllabic or logographic writing, where phonemic segmentation is presumably not necessary for learning to read and write. In fact, some reports claim that reading difficulty and disability are quite uncommon among children in Japan (Makita, 1968; Sakamoto, 1980, p. 23) and Taiwan (Kuo, 1978). Two of these reports are based on questionnaires given to teachers, however, so despite the authors' efforts at defining 'reading difficulty,' the results are not directly comparable to measures of reading difficulty in alphabetic writing systems. Moreover, cultural factors, such as reluctance to identify children as having difficulty, may have affected the results.

More research has been directed to the related question of whether readers of non-alphabetic scripts employ phonemic recoding. The evidence so far is mixed. Treiman, Baron and Luk (1981) found that while readers of English were less accurate in evaluating sentences containing homophones (e.g., 'A pair is a fruit.' [True/False]), readers of Chinese were unaffected by comparable homophony. Chu-Chang and Loritz (1977) and Tzeng, Hung, and Wang (1977) on the other hand, both found evidence of phonological representation in the reading of Chinese. The resolution suggested by Tzeng and Hung (1980) is that phonological representation operates in both perception and memory in the reading of English, but only in memory in the reading of Chinese. In any case, non-alphabetic writing systems may reduce segmentation difficulty at the level of the phoneme, at least for learners. Rozin, Poritsky and Sotsky (1971) and Rozin and Gleitman (1977) report success in teaching syllabaries to children who have had difficulty in learning to read and write alphabetically.

It would be interesting to gather evidence from other languages for less technical reasons as well. Our culture includes certain attitudes toward spelling and correctness in spelling; it would be interesting to learn through comparative studies what effect these attitudes may have on children's development. Some children create their own spellings quite readily, while others do not, partly because they attach more importance to correctness, evidently. To what extent do these differences reflect personality characteristics and to what extent do they reflect the differential learning of parental or cultural attitudes? One kind of evidence would be the development of children in other cultures.

Likewise, other countries employ different methods of instruction from those which are generally used here. Sometimes these methods challenge received opinion in our culture. For example, Ferguson (1971) notes that there are at least two features of literacy instruction in Ethiopia that would raise the eyebrows of experts in the United States: that children become literate in a language which they do not speak, and that in the process they typically do a great deal of memorization. Ferguson does not claim that these methods are optimal or even superior to those used in the United States, but he notes some indications that they are working better than we might expect.

For all of these reasons, then, the strong bias in the study of literacy development toward English in the United States or its cultural neighbors, has probably been a mistake. Even though it is natural and often productive to focus on one's own language, and even though English orthography presents interesting problems of its own, we may learn more about literacy development, even in English, by studying the process in several languages.

II Studies in other languages

The potential significance of studying children's spelling in languages other than English has not gone unnoticed. During the past decade, researchers have looked at phonological effects on beginning spelling in Dutch, French, German and Spanish (Table 4.1). Although these languages are all relatively close to English phonologically, they differ enough to answer some of the questions raised above. The studies have much in common: almost all used (at least) a dictation task in first grade (and in higher grades or the preschool as well), with the classroom teacher dictating words in sentence context as well as in isolation. The stimuli were selected for their phonological and morphological structure, including various vowels and consonants and various kinds of sequences. All in all, these investigations show that children create spellings in other languages which are either like those observed in English or which differ from the English spellings in ways that can usually be traced to the structure of the language. The studies certainly confirm that in order to understand children's development, even in English, we must look to other languages as well.

TABLE 4.1   *Studies of children's beginning spelling in languages other than English*

Language	Location	Investigator	Grades	n (approx.)
Dutch	Zutphen	Niski (1978)	1-2	143, 112
	Overasselt	van Rijnsoever (1979)	preschool-1	33, 54
French	Montreal	Gill (1980)	1-4	108
German	Osnabrück(?)	Castrup (1978)	1-2	1 class
	Schwaben	Eichler (1976)	preschool-4	n.a.
	Eichstätt	Temple, Schlicht and Henderson (1981)	1-4	130
Spanish	Dominican Republic	Temple (1978, 1980)	1-3	75

A Preconsonantal nasals

The studies of Dutch, French and Spanish have dealt with the spelling of nasals. Of these, Niski's was the first, the one with the largest sample, and the only one focussed solely on nasals. Niski elicited spellings of Dutch words with preconsonantal nasals from 255 children altogether: 143 in first grade and 112 in second grade. The children came from ten different schools in the area of Zutphen, in the eastern part of the Netherlands. A Dutch dialect study (Weijnen, 1966) gives no indication that the Zutphen pronunciation of nasals differs from that of other regions. Niski also conducted an experiment like the 'pointer' study in Read (1975, pp. 108-12), designed to determine where children locate the difference between the Dutch phonological counterparts of *bet* and *bent*.

Van Rijnsoever elicited spellings from fifty-four Dutch first graders; he also studied the spontaneous spellings of thirty-three preschoolers. The first graders were in Overasselt, a village in the southeastern region of the country.

Temple studied the spellings produced by first, second and third graders in the Dominican Republic, with about fifteen students in the first grade and thirty-five in each of the other two. In the twenty dictated words, Temple included various monophthongs and diphthongs, as well as consonants categorized by their position within a syllable, whether they correspond to a letter name, and whether they are 'ambiguous' because of phonological variation.

Gill studied the spelling of children in grades one through four of a private French-speaking school near Montreal, with an average of twenty-seven children per grade. The nineteen words which each teacher dictated included nine nasalized vowels.

1 Dutch

The first conclusion that we can draw from the work of Niski and van Rijnsoever is that the omission of preconsonantal nasals is approximately as frequent in Dutch as it is in English, and it is most frequent in the same phonological context. First graders in Niski's study omitted from 25 per cent to 38 per cent of preconsonantal nasals, and in van Rijnsoever's, from 15 per cent to 27 per cent, with the largest percentage in both studies occurring with nasals that followed a short vowel and preceded a homorganic voiceless consonant.

Niski also observed Dutch children's self-corrections: approximately 75 per cent of the self-corrections by first graders involved the nasal segment in a vowel-nasal-stop sequence, and about 85 per cent of these consisted of inserting nasal spellings where they had previously been omitted. Van Rijnsoever adds evidence from preschoolers: they omitted from 33 per cent to 50 per cent of preconsonantal nasals, depending on phonological context, or about double the frequency among first graders.

This agreement between English and Dutch observations tends to disconfirm explanations which depend on some circumstances in just one language or country. For instance, because Dutch standard orthography differs substantially from that of English, we may conclude that the omission of preconsonantal nasals does not arise from some orthographic quirk of English, such as a few frequent but misleading words. Likewise, the Dutch confirmation seems to rule out certain dialect influences, such as the raised and sometimes nasalized /æ/ that one hears in various parts of the United States. In short, of the many conceivable explanations for the non-representation of preconsonantal nasals, the more circumstantial ones are strongly disconfirmed by the simple fact that children in different languages and cultures spell in the same way.

The Dutch studies also help to establish the phonological environments in which nasals are least likely to be represented. Niski and van Rijnsoever considered three factors: the length of the preceding vowel, the voicing of the following consonant, and the agreement in place of articulation (homorganicity) of the nasal and the consonant. On vowel length, Niski and van Rijnsoever reach the same conclusion: that by itself it is not a significant influence on the spelling of the nasal. Only van Rijnsoever takes up voicing; he finds that a voiceless following consonant makes it less likely that the nasal will be represented (p. < .05), but the difference is entirely among words with short vowels, so it appears that vowel length and consonant voicing interact.

Most interesting is the effect of homorganicity, which cannot be studied in English, since all syllable-final sequences of nasal + consonant must be homorganic (as in *bend*, **benb*). Even within Dutch, one might expect that any effect would be attenuated, since a sequence of vowel-nasal-[non-homorganic] stop may actually be pronounced (or perceived) with an epenthetic homorganic stop. For example, Dutch *hemd* may be pronounced either [hɛmt] or [hɛmpt], Dutch *lengte* may be pronounced either [lɛŋtə] or [lɛŋktə], and so on. Despite this variation, homorganicity led to significantly more nasal-omissions in van Rijnsoever's study (p. < .02), although it made no significant difference in Niski's. In sum, none of the three factors (length, voicing or homorganicity) had a large effect on nasal omission, although the latter two were significant factors in van Rijnsoever's data.

a Nasals versus clusters of other consonants Another issue on which the Dutch studies are enlightening is the relation between the omission of preconsonantal nasals and that of other consonants within clusters. Read (1971, 1975) viewed the nasal sequences as different from syllable-final *-st* or *-ld* clusters, for example, because he found a large difference in the frequency of omissions. In his sample of young children's spelling, 30 per cent of preconsonantal nasals were omitted, whereas only 3 per cent of *-st* clusters and 4 per cent of *-ld* clusters were similarly reduced. Marcel (1980), on the other hand, groups all such cluster reductions together because he finds that they all characterize the spelling of adults and children with spelling difficulty. This difference is important to the explanation of the nasal-omission phenomenon: is it one instance of a general difficulty in segmenting clusters or is it conditioned by properties such as brief duration which are unique to the nasals? Fricatives and laterals in consonant clusters are not particularly brief, and they are not encoded upon the preceding vowel in the manner or to the extent that nasals are, via nasalization. These two accounts are not incompatible, however; the omission of pre-consonantal nasals in beginning spelling may be one instance of a general difficulty in segmentation, but a particularly frequent and persistent one because of the phonetic character of those nasals.

It turns out that the Dutch studies provide some support for this mixed view. Both Niski and van Rijnsoever found that in syllable-final clusters, nasals are omitted about twice as frequently as other consonants. Niski then asked whether it is the same children who reduce initial consonant clusters and omit preconsonantal nasals. He found that in *stoomt, steunt, klomp, kraampje* and *gromt*, children who omitted a nasal were more than twice as likely to reduce the initial cluster in the same word. Overall, children who omitted nasals in these words also reduced the initial cluster 49 per cent of the time, while other children did so only 21 per cent of the time. Niski made a similar observation (pp. 82-3) in comparing children's ability to locate the difference between /buk/ and /bruk/

and between /ent/ and /et/: for the most part, it was the same children who located each difference on neither the stop nor the vowel, but between the two. As Niski points out (p. 12), the initial clusters may be easier to segment both because they are in a more accessible position within the word and because their segments are phonetically more distinct (i.e., longer, not homorganic, and less thoroughly encoded upon the vowel).

b Individual differences   Niski also conducted a partial replication of the 'pointer' experiment in Read (1975), with some interesting variations in procedure. In Niski's version, children who had omitted nasals in the dictation were later asked to spell the same words on a playing board using cardboard letters. If asked to spell *klomp*, for example, these children usually selected KLOP. Then the experimenter introduced the word *klop*, i.e., the other member of a minimal pair, without the nasal. After checking on the child's ability to read back the word which he/she had spelled and to pronounce both words, the experimenter gave the child a pointer to be placed on the spelling KLOP to show where the difference is between the two words.

As noted in Chapter 1, Read (1975) found that children who placed the pointer in a consistent position fell into just two groups: those who generally represented the nasal and placed the pointer at that location, and those who did not represent the nasal and placed the pointer on the vowel. Read took this as evidence that children who do not yet represent these nasals, but who are able to perform consistently on this explicit segmentation task, generally perceive the vowel as the main difference in such pairs of words. This perception is also phonetically accurate.

In addition to these two kinds of responses, however, Niski found two others: children who did not represent the nasal in their spelling but nonetheless consistently pointed to the space between the vowel and the consonant as the location of the difference in sound, and children who pointed to the consonant. Perhaps these latter children regarded the difference between *klop* and *klomp* as /p/ versus /mp/, i.e., they regarded the nasal + stop sequence as a single perceptual unit. In terms of articulatory gestures which we can feel, this sequence does form a unit; it is a single movement of the lips, and we cannot feel the intervening movement of the velum.

Niski's results remind us that children may vary in the way they segment words into speech sounds, especially as they learn to read and write. When children begin to sense, perhaps vaguely, that syllables have an internal structure, they may have differing conceptions of this structure, rather like the perception of an ambiguous picture. In fact, segmentation of speech, which is a continuous phonetic form, *is* ambiguous: the nasalization which distinguishes *klop* from *klomp* is superimposed upon the vowel and the /p/; only in spelling (and in the percepts of literate speakers) is it a discrete unit. Acoustically, the nasalization goes with the vowel; kinesthetically, it goes with the consonant.

This account of children's beginning spelling raises important questions for further research:

– Is this individual variation truly in segmentation, rather than in a response bias? Is there evidence from other tasks that children differ in their segmentation of such sequences?
– What difference in the task (or the language) might account for the fact that Niski found four kinds of responses while Read found only two? (For each of the three possible locations, Niski found children who consistently chose that location.)
– Do children differ individually in their segmentation of other consonant clusters as well, and is there any relation between their segmentation of the VNC sequences and that of other clusters? For instance, does a child who locates the difference between *bet* and *bent* at the vowel do the same for *pet* and *pest*?
– Is there any developmental or predictive significance to the differences in segmentation? For example, does segmentation on an acoustic basis develop later than that on an articulatory basis? Does one segmentation lead more readily toward the adult judgment and standard spelling?

In general, as we examine children's literacy development in detail, we need to be alert to this kind of individual variation. Most previous research, emphasizing treatment variables over subject variables, has probably overlooked variation in specific strategies, even when revealing large differences in overall literacy development.

2 Spanish

Temple (1978) dictated no words containing preconsonantal nasals to first graders in Spanish (Dominican Republic). There were three such words in the dictation at second and third grades, two with /mb/ (*bombon* and *invierno*) and one with /nč/ (*hinchado*). Second graders omitted these two nasals 16 per cent and 5 per cent of the time respectively, while third graders did so 9 per cent and 6 per cent of the time. A much larger number of errors had to do with whether assimilation is represented in spelling: both *bombon* and *invierno* are pronounced with /mb/ but only the former is spelled with *mb*. Omissions were the second largest category of non-standard spellings of nasals, after under- and over-representation of assimilation, as in BONBON and IMBIERNO.

3 French

Gill (1980) provides another perspective on children's representation of nasals in her study of children's spelling of Montreal French. The words which teachers in the monolingual French-speaking school dictated included all four of the nasalized vowels of French, two of them occurring in both preconsonantal and word-final position.

Gill does not provide phonetic transcriptions of the stimuli as pronounced in the classroom; indeed, the pronunciation probably varied somewhat from one teacher to another. We must therefore represent the words in a broad transcription. In particular, we cannot know whether in a word such as *nombre*, the actual pronunciations included a consonantal nasal of some duration after the nasalized vowel. The words dictated were the following:

magasins	/magəzɛ̃/
humble	/œ̃blə/
nombre	/nõbʁ/
conduit	/kõdɥi/
changeant	/šãžã/
pinceaux	/pɛ̃so/
enfants	/ãfã/

In only about 6 per cent of the spellings did the first graders (n = 28) fail to represent the nasalization of the vowel with the letter M or N. Second graders omitted even fewer (2 per cent) of these markers, and the third and fourth graders omitted none. There was no difference between the preconsonantal and the word-final environments. In short, there is little indication in this study of French of the nasal omission which is such a salient and robust phenomenon in children's spelling of English and Dutch.

Phonetically, words with preconsonantal nasalized vowels in French are similar to words with preconsonantal 'nasals' in English and Dutch:

French	nombre	[nõbʀ]
English	number	[nʌ̃(m)bɚ]
Dutch	panter	[pã(n)tɚ]

In fact, any difference in nasalization is toward brief nasal consonants in English and Dutch, but not in French. Why, then, is it French-speaking children who more frequently represent the nasalization?

It might seem that the phonemic status of nasalized vowels in French accounts for this difference in spelling. If children strive to represent just the phonemic contrasts in their language, then since nasalized vowels contrast phonemically with oral vowels in French, children should more or less consistently represent them. This explanation will not suffice, however, for the simple reason that preconsonantal vowel nasalization is phonemically significant in all three languages. English *bet* [bɛt] contrasts with *bent* [bɛ̃(n)t] in much the same way that French *mets* [mɛ] contrasts with *main* [mɛ̃], namely in the absence or presence of nasalization on the vowel. Moreover, in all three languages the standard spelling of that nasalized vowel is similar: as a vowel followed by *n*.

If the phonemic status of vowel nasalization cannot account for the cross-language difference in spelling, then perhaps the distribution of nasalization can do so. Nasalized vowels are found in more phonological environments in French, after all. It turns out, however, that the only real difference in distribution is that French has syllable-final nasalized vowels, as in *bon* [bõ], whereas Dutch and English do not. Otherwise, all three languages have syllable-initial nasal consonants, nasalized vowels followed by nasal consonants, and the preconsonantal nasalized vowels discussed here. (There are other differences, such as the occurrence of a palatal nasal in French, but these have no direct relevance to the spelling of preconsonantal nasals.) In all three languages, children would produce essentially standard spellings of nasals if they simply inferred that nasals at the beginnings of syllables are spelled *n* or *m*, and all the rest are spelled as a vowel followed by *n* or *m*, regardless of whether the nasalization is primarily vocalic or consonantal. (Again, this spelling rule would have to be more complicated to encompass palatal and velar nasals, but the core process would be unaffected.) Young children do generally represent phonemic distinctions, and nasalized vowels do differ in status and distribution between French and English (or Dutch), but those facts are not sufficient to explain the difference in first graders' spelling of nasals. In seeking other explanations, we may learn more about the role of segmentation and categorization in beginning spelling.

The difference in the phonemic status of nasalization may help to account for the difference in beginning spelling via adults' awareness of language and its effect on instruction. French-speaking teachers are of course aware that nasalized vowels exist in their language and that there are spelling conventions for representing them. English- and Dutch-speaking teachers do not know that the same is true of their languages. American teachers may know that their students produce spellings such as DOT for *don't*, but they usually do not realize how frequently such spellings occur or that they occur specifically for nasals that precede consonants. Still less, of course, do most American teachers realize that such nasals are really nasalized vowels, and that that is the reason for the spelling pattern. Teachers of French-speaking children (and their textbooks and curricula) explicitly teach the spelling of nasalized vowels, while English-speaking teachers treat them as unremarkable sequences of vowel plus nasal consonant. It may be that the French teachers' awareness, communicated to the children, leads to more consistent spelling of nasalized vowels, an effect of adults' beliefs about language on children's learning.

a Possible effects of syllable structure   A difference in syllable structure among these languages may also help to explain children's (non)representation of nasals. In French, the canonical syllable is an open one, i.e., a syllable ending in a vowel. Léon (1966, pp. 15-16) estimates that about 80 per cent of French syllables are open, although he does not say whether this refers to types or tokens.

Hyphenation in written French reflects this preference; *saucisson* is hyphenated *sau-cisson* rather than *sauc-isson*, for instance. In normal speech, there are probably no phonetic signals of syllable structure where the division might be made in more than one way. That is, there are no cues that divide French *ici* [i-si] rather than [is-i]. However, both children and adults can produce such divisions in overly slow (unnatural) pronunciation, and in doing so, French speakers seem to favor open syllables.

It turns out that all the nasalized vowels in Gill's stimuli were in open syllables, both medially as in *pinceaux* /pɛ̃-so] and finally as in *magasins* /magəzɛ̃/. On the other hand, the preconsonantal nasals which children so frequently omit in spelling English and Dutch are primarily in closed syllables. All the monosyllables (e.,g., *bent*) are closed, and for morphological reasons, one might argue that some of the polysyllables are, too (e.g., *bumpy* and *stinker*). There is a plausible relation between syllable structure and spelling in that if the nasal is homorganic with a following consonant in the same syllable, it may be more likely to be omitted in favor of the oral consonant, which is a stop or fricative and therefore relatively salient. Recall that van Rijnsoever found significantly more omissions before homorganic consonants. This effect can not be tested in English, where consonants must be homorganic with a preceding nasal within a syllable, but it would explain the more frequent omissions in English than in French, assuming primarily closed syllables in the former and primarily open ones in the latter. There are nasalized vowels in closed syllables in French, as in *hampe* /ã:p/ and *pampe* /põ:p/, which might be used to test this effect.

4 Conclusions about nasals

Although the evidence is by no means complete, one can draw some conclusions from the study of this one spelling across three languages. The Dutch studies confirm the generality of the pattern. They strongly reinforce the hypothesis that the omission of nasals in this position is attributable to the phonetic form, rather than to orthography, dialect or instruction. The Dutch studies also help to clarify the roles of vowel length and consonant voicing in conditioning these omissions, and they show that homorganicity may be a conditioning factor, one which could not have been investigated in English. Also in Niski's and van Rijnsoever's work is a strong suggestion that the omission of preconsonantal nasals may be simply one instance of the general segmentation difficulty that gives rise to the reduction of other consonant clusters in beginning spelling, but a special instance because of the phonetic structure of these VNC sequences, namely the nasalization of the vowel, the extremely brief duration of the nasal (if any), and the homorganic articulation of the nasal and consonant.

Niski's 'pointer' experiment gives us a glimpse of individual variation in the way in which children segment such sequences. Such variation may be of great importance to any detailed understanding of the beginning of literacy. We need to know, for example, whether a child's use of one spelling pattern is predictable from his or her use of any other, and whether patterns such as the omission of preconsonantal nasals occur in an all-or-nothing manner that suggests the learning of a generalization. Read (1975, p. 106) gives some evidence for this latter possibility. In general, if we think of spelling as a problem that children solve in different ways, it is both scientifically and educationally important to find out what knowledge and cognitive abilities account for the different approaches.

Gill's study of French, on the other hand, shows that this spelling pattern differs across languages in response to differences in phonological structure, i.e., that what matters is not only speech sounds, but their role within a phonological system. Beginning spelling depends on segmenting and categorizing speech sounds, not merely perceiving and representing them. Sapir, writing in the first issue of *Language* (1925), similarly observed that speech sounds are not discrete units in a list, but occupy positions in relation to one another. 'This is the inner configuration of the sound system of the language, the intuitive "placing" of the sounds with reference to one another.' Compared with the basic interpretation of vocal behavior as speech (e.g., the interpretation of a hissing action as the speech sound /s/), this relational pattern is 'more elusive and of correspondingly greater significance for the linguist.' In young children's spelling, this elusive configuration sometimes becomes observable.

B Consonants

In the studies of preconsonantal nasals, we see one phenomenon in four languages. The same studies and others contain cross-linguistic data on children's spelling of a range of other consonants. Let us look first at a type of spelling that appears early in children's spelling of English, namely spellings that are heavily influenced by letter-names. Temple (1978, 1980) reports one example in Spanish: the use of the letter H to represent /č/ in the words *pecho* and *choque*. At the first grade, 17 per cent of the spellings that Temple elicited were of this sort, presumably including PEHO and HOQUE. As in English, the name of the letter *h* in Spanish (/ače/) contains /č/, but the digraph *ch* is often treated as a letter, named /če/. Also as in English, the issue is complicated by the fact that the standard spelling is *ch*: the spelling H might represent the influence of the letter-name, a reduction of the standard spelling, or both.

Gill (1980) provides an example from her study of French-speaking children which also coincides with both a letter-name and a standard spelling, although she does not label it as such, namely the use of J to represent /ž/ in *changeant*, for instance. J is named /ži/ in French, but it is also a standard spelling for /ž/ in certain positions, as in *jardin*. The frequency of this spelling actually increased from 11 per cent in grade one to 17 per cent in grade two (but only 3 per cent in grade three), suggesting an influence of standard spelling rather than of the letter-name. Thus two apparent examples of letter-name spellings in other languages are both confounded with standard spelling. It remains to be seen whether the influence of letter-names is especially strong in English because of the emphasis on letter-names in primary teaching.

Staczek reports an influence of English letter-names on the spelling of Spanish vowels by Spanish-English bilinguals in the Miami area. This effect is contrary to standard Spanish spelling but consistent with English letter-names, namely the use of *e* to represent /i/ and *a* to represent /e/. Staczek and Aid (1981, pp. 152-3) and Staczek (1982, pp. 143-4) cite several examples of each of these spellings, reporting the frequency of each but not the relative frequency. Note that a parallel effect on the other three Spanish vowel phonemes could not be observed: using English letter-names as a guide to spelling /u/ and /o/ would lead to *u* and *o*, which are standard Spanish spellings, while English letter-names give no direct clue to the spelling of /a/. The problem with Staczek's study for our purposes is that the sample included bilinguals from kindergarten through to university, and the reports do not differentiate by age.

Another characteristic noted in two of the languages is that of representing clusters of two consonants with a single letter. This reduction is like the omission of preconsonantal nasals, but generalized to other consonants in other positions. One of the sources is Temple's (1978, 1980) study of spelling in Dominican Spanish, but since all of the cluster simplifications (except possibly that of preconsonantal nasals) appear to be dialect effects, they will be taken up under that heading, below. Van Rijnsoever (1979) makes the distribution of cluster reductions in Dutch quite clear: it is the inner consonant which is not represented, i.e., the second one in an initial cluster and the first in a final cluster. For example, van Rijnsoever (1979, Table 9) shows that in spelling initial /kl-/ clusters, first graders omitted the /l/ 31 per cent of the time, but the /k/ less than 1 per cent. Conversely, in spelling a final /-ft/ cluster, they omitted the /f/ 13 per cent of the time but never omitted the /t/. Overall, consonants in the vulnerable positions were omitted from 10 per cent to 31 per cent of the time by first graders.

Some characteristics of children's spelling in any language are phonetic only in the sense of ignoring non-phonetic aspects of standard spelling. For instance, Gill (1980) notes that children often failed to write doubled consonants and other 'silent' letters in French. Virtually every study notes the use of standard spellings in nonstandard contexts, as in a German child's use of F and SCH in FARSCHTAND for *verstand* (Temple, Schlicht and Henderson, 1981).

Two such spelling patterns noted by Temple deserve comment, however. In German, Temple *et al.* (1981) observed that children frequently spell devoiced final consonants with the phonetically-appropriate letter, rather than the morphologically-appropriate one used in standard spelling. Thus, first graders write *verstand* with a final T 48 per cent of the time. What seems at first surprising is that they write *halb* and *grob* with a P, and *stieg* with a K, far less often: 3 per cent, 6 per cent and 10 per cent, respectively. Temple *et al.* attribute this contrast to the fact that some cases in which final [t] is spelled -*d* are in inflectional suffixes, 'and therefore . . . subject to morphological constraints in addition to those associated with phonological changes and phoneme-grapheme relationships' (p. 13). Another way to look at it is in terms of standard spelling: final -*t* is simply far more frequent than -*p* or -*k*. One reverse dictionary of German (Mater, 1970) contains only about 210 entries with final -*p*, about 3060 entries with final -*k*, but about 19,000 entries with a final -*t*. For these three final letters, relative frequency in children's spelling is parallel to that in standard spelling. Moreover, it is the best readers among the first graders who most clearly display this parallelism, a fact which tends to confirm the influence of standard spelling. Of course, both complexity and standard spelling may contribute to this pattern in the beginning spelling of German.

Temple (1978, pp. 98-9) observed that children in the Dominican Republic chose C far more often than Q as a spelling for /k/, although both are standard spellings in Spanish (in different contexts). In so doing, they greatly preferred the more frequent standard spelling to the one that has /k/ in its letter-name. Again, even first graders appear to have a sense of what is frequent in standard spelling. In part, the influence of standard spelling in Temple's observations of both German and Spanish may reflect the fact that in both cases, he was prevented from studying the youngest children. In the Dominican Republic, the teachers refused to allow the less advanced first graders to participate, and in Germany, Temple was not able to collect data until the second half of the school year. This problem has been frequent in the literature; it is harder to arrange to work with preschool children, and researchers are less likely to begin collecting data early in a school year. As a result, we badly need more observations of children's earlier spelling in languages other than English. It is at the beginning, after all, that the most revealing nonstandard spellings occur.

Finally, in addition to the preconsonantal nasals, there are other patterns in children's spelling of Dutch, French, German and Spanish exactly like those observed in English. Van Rijnsoever (1979) confirms for Dutch the observation (see Chapter 1) that children are likely to omit a vowel spelling in representing the syllables /əl/, /əm/, /ən/, and /ɚ/, i.e., syllables with (potentially syllabic) sonorants. The Dutch children omitted the vowels before a sonorant about 20 per cent of the time. In Eichler's

(1976) data from German, there are also many examples of this omission: KASN and KSNT for *Kasten*, STEMPLN for *stampeln*, and KATN for *Garten*, for instance. Evidently, children treat sonorants differently from obstruents; that is, /əl/ and /ət/ and spelled as if they had different syllabic forms. The syllabic forms may indeed be different; the sonorant may constitute a syllable without a vowel, depending in part on whether the sonorant is homorganic with the preceding consonant. Whether the children's spellings are accurate in phonetic detail, omitting the vowel in spelling just when no vowel occurs in speech, is not yet known.

Several of the observed spellings reflect characteristics of the children's dialects. For example, in his study of Dominican Spanish, Temple (1978, 1980) reports that children omit /s/ in spelling *triste* and omit the final /d/ in *verdad* and *libertad*. These speech sounds in these positions are often not pronounced in Caribbean Spanish, and in Dominican Spanish in particular (Canfield, 1981, pp. 45-7; Terrell, 1977), so no doubt the children were representing their dialect accurately. Similarly, Temple reports that the /r/ in *verdad* and *libertad* is omitted about 22 per cent of the time overall (about 35 per cent by first graders). From 8 per cent to 25 per cent of the first and second graders spelled these /r/'s with an L. In Caribbean Spanish, an /r/ in this position may be produced as /l/ or even as a semivowel (/j/), so once again the spellings probably correspond to pronunciation. Staczek and Aid (1981) also observed /r/ spelled L among their Spanish/English bilinguals; that spelling and /l/ spelled R occur nine times in a list of fifteen spellings which they attribute to dialect variation.

A dialect-based spelling which appears bizarre is LL for /č/, reported by Temple (1980). Temple's account is that /j/, sometimes spelled LL in Spanish, may be quite strident in Dominican Spanish, so that the children relate it to /č/. That is, the spelling of a palatal fricative (in Dominican) is applied to a palato-alveolar affricate.

Eichler cites several effects of the Swabian dialect of the children he observed. Among consonants, perhaps the most frequent examples reflect the tendency to produce voiced stops where standard German has voiceless ones: REGENDROPFEN and REGENTROBFEN for *Regentropfen*, BRASSELN for *prasseln*, and SCHALLTED for *schaltet*, for instance. Children also overgeneralized in their attempt to undo this effect: they wrote LEBENTICH for *lebendich* and WENTE for *Wande*, for example. Eichler notes that the child's own pronunciation is at least as relevant to the spelling as that of the teacher. He suggests that the process of creative spelling includes an inner recreation of the speech segments ('die innere Neuproduktion der Lauteinheiten,' p. 255). As a result, the child's dialect may be reflected in spelling, even where it differs from what was dictated.

C Vowels

The most extensive and interesting observations of the spelling of vowels come from van Rijnsoever (1979), for both preschool and first-grade Dutch children. He first asks whether these children tend to spell tense/lax pairs of vowels alike, as American children do (see pp. 5-11). The first graders' spellings are mostly standard (or standard but in the wrong context), so the focus is on the preschoolers. The pairs of interest are /e/-/I/ and /O/-/ʌ/. These are of course not the same as the pairs in English, but van Rijnsoever cites good phonetic evidence that they bear the same relation as the English pairs. As noted above, it is this potential for studying different phonetic and phonological systems that motivates the cross-linguistic studies. Van Rijnsoever's conclusion is:

The spellings U for /O/, E for /I/, and I for /e/ are each the most frequent nonstandard spellings. They support the hypothesis [that the preschool children will spell the tense/lax counterparts alike]. [pp. 180-1; translated by CR.]

Next, van Rijnsoever takes up the relation between rounded vowels and unrounded ones. When children try to spell a rounded vowel but produce a nonstandard spelling, is it a spelling of another rounded vowel or an unrounded one, and if the latter, are the vowels related in height, backness or some other feature? He first observes that Dutch preschoolers, like American ones, tend to spell back rounded vowels alike; by far the most frequent nonstandard spelling for /u/ is O, which is the standard spelling for /o/ and /ɔ/. He then shows that this is not likely to be merely an abbreviated form of the standard spelling for /u/ (*oe*), on the grounds that children rarely reduce other digraphic spellings to a single letter, and that when the preschoolers do so, they do not consistently produce either the first or the second letter. The inference is that like their American counterparts, Dutch children group back rounded vowels together. Van Rijnsoever then questions this conclusion, however, noting that children who spell /u/ with O spell /o/ with both O and OO, both of which are standard, but in different contexts. That is, if children use a spelling of /o/ when they create one for /u/, why do they not use *both* of the frequent spellings of /o/? As van Rijnsoever says, a study of individual strategies might be revealing.

Finally, van Rijnsoever takes up the relation between rounded and unrounded front vowels, a relation that cannot be studied in English. He concludes:

> None of the spellings for front rounded vowels occurs as a spelling
> for front unrounded ones or vice-versa. . . . Judging from the
> spellings, the children sharply distinguish these two types of
> vowels. (p. 184; translated by CR.]

He goes on to suggest that among front vowels the primary (most salient) grouping is on the basis of rounding. To a speaker of English, at least, this suggestion has a good deal of intuitive appeal, and it accords with the fact that phonological processes tend to affect these two groups separately. The general 'map' suggested by van Rijnsoever's study, then, is that front and back rounded vowels each form a cohesive group, distinct from each other.

D Beginning spelling in a 'regular' orthography

Anyone familiar with primary schooling in English-speaking countries cannot help noticing a practical problem encountered in both the Dutch and Spanish studies: that by the latter part of the first-grade year, there are hardly enough nonstandard spellings to support this kind of investigation, at least for some major classes of speech sounds. Both van Rijnsoever and Temple comment on this fact. Standard spelling in both languages is phonemically regular (in the usual sense), with the obvious reservation that no orthography can correspond to varied dialects equally well. Van

Heuven (1980) points out some inconsistencies in Dutch spelling, but these are few in number and relatively transparent compared with those in English. In van Rijnsoever's studies, for example, first graders would have spelled /e/ correctly more than 90 per cent of the time if they had only mastered the rule that tense vowels are spelled with a single letter in an open syllable but with a geminate in a closed one; i.e., that /e/ is spelled *e* in *leger* and *ee* in *leeg*. This is clearly not the stuff of which persistent, time-consuming spelling difficulties are made. Kyöstiö (1980) suggests that learning to read Finnish is facilitated at the early stages by the regular orthography.

Temple (1980) is quite explicit in rejecting the inference that orthographies should be reformed to be more like that of Spanish. In fact, he suggests (pp. 177-8) that the Dominican children were misled into relying exclusively on the phonemic predictabiliity of Spanish spelling, thus making errors in the cases where it fails. In any case, there is a great difference between observing that an orthography is relatively easy for a child learning to spell and concluding that it is optimal for an adult reader. We know just enough to suspect that what is good for one is not necessarily good for the other. Even if that major question were answered, there would still be the practical fact that spelling reform in English has failed for 200 years (Venezky, 1980), and that redesigning an orthography for a language as far-flung and varied as English is no trivial task. In short, there may be no single optimal orthography for a language; what is optimal may depend on the user's knowledge and his or her dialect.

The studies of beginning spelling across languages have demonstrated their value; they provide a strong test of inferences made on the basis of English, and they have revealed aspects of the process that are hidden in English. However, these studies have not yet fulfilled their potential. We need studies of other languages, chosen with informed attention to their phonology and ortho-graphy, and we need more studies of the beginnings of spelling, the stage at which revealing 'errors' are most frequent.

Cross-linguistic evidence is essential to a real understanding of beginning spelling. What we can observe in one language depends on its phonetics, phonology and orthography, including even such seemingly minor details as its letter-names. Each language poses certain puzzles for the beginning speller, while making other choices easy. Only by studying a range of languages can we have much confidence in our hypotheses about why children make the choices that they do.

5 Toward a theory of spelling development

The goal of this chapter is to place beginning spelling in its context: the conceptions of written language that precede spelling itself, the cognitive development that underlies it, and the reading skills which develop alongside it. Only by understanding creative spelling in this context can we lay the foundations for a theory of how spelling develops.

I Foundations

The next two sections of the chapter examine two precursors to spelling: children's early conceptions of what is represented in written language and their ability to identify individual speech sounds. Then we examine the development of general cognition and reading ability, alongside that of spelling. Finally, we outline a general conception of how spelling develops, combining the implications of creative spelling with findings from experimental studies. The chapter concludes with some suggestions for teachers and parents who wish to facilitate children's early development in spelling.

A Young children's conceptions of written language

Clearly, invented spelling is not the beginning of the process of learning to write. It rests on some general cognitive foundations, such as conceptions of the nature and purpose of writing, and some specific ones, such as the knowledge that spellings correspond to speech sounds. We cannot really understand the development of spelling without seeing the growth of this prior knowledge. A few investigators have found ways to do just that and have revealed a rich fabric of early development in conceptions of writing.

Clay, in *What Did I Write?* (1975), describes five-year-olds' writing during their first two months of school. She finds no discernible sequence of acquisition, but does find that most children begin by inventing scribbles or mock writing before they begin to recognize real letters. Often the first words they learn to write are their own names, beginning with the initial letter and sometimes including their family name. Clay notes that at this stage their knowledge of words is simultaneously approximate and specific: e.g., Ian writes his name IAN and refuses to recognize *Ian* as equivalent. Jenny writes *Jehhy* and refuses to accept *Jenny* (p. 15).

Soon after children learn to write a few letters, they discover repetition, writing long strings of letters or words, and apparently deriving much satisfaction from this activity. Later they realize that long passages may also be produced by arranging and rearranging all of the letters or words that they know. Most of these sequences turn out not to be real words, of course. Nevertheless, children know that writing is purposeful and that grown-ups can read, so they expect adults to be able to identify them. Only later do they realize that writing corresponds to speech in specific ways (p. 53).

Somewhat later, children enjoy taking inventory of their knowledge, in lists of letters (alphabets), words and names. This may become a structuring activity, listing matched upper- and lower-case letters, contrasting pairs, major classes, or similar forms, such as MW or AH.

An apparent difficulty for many children is the directionality of writing. When copying or tracing they frequently do not discriminate backward from forward writing, or even upside down from right side up. When a word shows through from a page underneath the one being written on, a child will often trace it without hesitation, whatever its orientation.

Clay asked children to 'read with your finger' and found that any direction is possible: left to right, right to left, top to bottom, bottom to top, and even snaking across a page in alternate directions. She points out that the direction of writing is an arbitrary convention; each of the directions has been used in some writing system. She believes that children learn the conventional direction after about six months of schooling, but then some children reverse it occasionally, perhaps just for fun. Before it is learned, directionality can also be violated when there is no room at the end of a line or page to finish a message. Then many children simply fill in the margin and other empty spaces on the page with the leftover words or parts of words. Clay suggests that the difficulty of learning to place spaces between words is related to learning directionality.

Lavine (1977) studied preschoolers' concepts of writing. She expected to see progressive differentiation of writing from other marks and symbols, e.g., of pictorial forms from nonpictorial ones, then further differentiation among linear nonpictorial forms, perhaps only in the context of a book or magazine, then adding criteria such as horizontal orientation, followed by identification of individual units that make up writing.

In a pilot experiment, Lavine showed twenty-three varied graphic displays to children aged from three to six years old. The displays included line drawings, geometric figures, letters, words, script, artificial letters, numbers, scribbles that resembled signatures, nonRoman letters and various lines. All of the three-year-olds distinguished pictures from writing, but not various types of writing from each other. Some four-year-olds further distinguished between writing-like scribbles and writing. Some five-year-olds distinguished numbers from letters. All of the children always included in 'writing' all Roman letters and script. By age five the children could recognize writing quite well, even though none of them could read. They learned first that writing is not pictorial, then that it is linear, then horizontal, and finally that it consists of Roman characters.

In her main study, Lavine increased the number of displays to thirty-five, of the same types as before. She tested forty-five preschoolers (fifteen each of three-, four- and five-year-olds) in Ithaca, New York; the sample was balanced for sex and socioeconomic status. Even though none of the children could read, many knew the names of some letters. By age three all of the children could differentiate writing from pictures. Of displays of conventional (Roman) letters, 86 per cent were classified as writing by the three-year-olds, 90 per cent by the four-year-olds, and 96 per cent by five-year-olds. In general, the results were like those of the pilot study.

Children looked for three general characteristics of writing: linearity, multiplicity and variety of symbols. Of these, linearity had a slight but statistically significant effect. Only the three-year-olds required multiplicity (more than one or two symbols per word), from which Lavine infers that the choice of symbol becomes more important than the number of symbols. As for variety, at all three ages children more often judged TOODLE to be writing than TTTTTT, for example.

i.e.

One class of signs shared no features with alphabetic writing; it consisted of Mayan motifs and Chinese characters. All of the children judged these not to be writing. It would be interesting to elicit judgments from Chinese, Arabic and other children whose writing systems employ nonRoman script to see if there are any criteria of writing shared by all. Apparently, children learn at an early age (and without instruction) to recognize some salient properties of the local writing system. We need to know which properties are salient in the various systems and what these properties may have in common.

In a different way, Ferreiro (1978) also showed that by the time children enter school, they already have a quite well-developed notion of what writing is. She interviewed sixty-eight four-, five- and six-year-olds in Buenos Aires. They were from either highly literate middle-class families or from working-class families with very low incomes. The four- and five-year-olds were enrolled in nursery schools which gave them no instruction in writing or reading. The six-year-olds were in the first few weeks of their first year of school. None of them knew how to read.

The task was designed to reveal a child's idea of the correspondences between segments of a written sentence and those of the spoken form. Ferreiro wrote out a sentence for a child and read it aloud, then asked the child to 'read' it back and to point out various words and phrases. The sentences were simple, containing a transitive verb and two noun phrases, each with a noun and an article (definite or indefinite). Each set of sentences contained several styles of print: all capitals, lower-case letters and cursive. In addition, they were either normally segmented or run together without spaces (p. 29):

ELOSOCOMEMIEL (thebeareatshoney)
PAPA PATEA LA PELOTA (papa kicks the ball)
la nena come un caramelo [cursive] (the girl eats a sweet)

Ferreiro found that the responses fell into six categories in developmental sequence, as follows:

1   The youngest children believed that only nouns are written. When the experimenter pointed out that there were more segments in the sentence than the two nouns which they had named, and then asked what the rest of the segments referred to, the children happily added other nouns which were appropriate to the context. For example, for *la nena compro un caramelo*, after locating 'nena' and 'carmelo' somewhere, the child added 'almacen' (shop) or 'kiosco' (stand). Ferreiro's interpretation is that the written text is conceived of at first as representing the people and objects referred to in the utterance, rather than the utterance itself.

2   The child finds the entire utterance in one fragment of the text, and fills in other contextually appropriate sentences for the rest of the segments. For example, a five-year-old girl segmented *la nena come un caramelo* as follows: she read 'Comi caramelo' (I ate a sweet) in *la nena*, 'Comi chocolate' (I ate chocolate) in *come un*, and 'Comi galletita y comi un chupetin' (I ate a cookie and I ate a lollipop) in *caramelo*.

3   The child finds it impossible to segment the utterance in any way corresponding to the text. He may even point to several different places in the text, or to the entire text, for one particular word. It seems that only entire utterances are written down, never individual words. For example, a five-year-old insisted that neither 'miel', nor 'come', nor 'come miel' could be found anywhere in the text: only 'Oso come miel' could be.

4   Nouns (both subject and object) are written, in separate segments, but the verb is not. At best, the verb can be written with its object, e.g., 'come miel', but never alone. For example, a four-year-old read 'caramelo' in *la nena*, 'nena' in *compro*, and 'compro un caramelo' in *un caramelo*.

5   Everything but the articles is written down. Children at this stage appear to believe either that the article is one syllable of the noun or that it is nothing. At least one four-year-old felt that two letters are insufficient: 'I tell you that with two letters you can't read. Don't put them like that . . . so far from the others.'

6   Everything that is said (read) is written. Given that the children in the study could not read, this segmentation is a

rather difficult accomplishment. From the example given by Ferreiro it seems that the child counted the position in the sentence of a given word. That is, when asked to point to 'caremelo' in *la nena come un caramelo*, a six-year-old said the sentence to herself, visually following the words, and came up with the correct position.

At no earlier point did it seem to matter whether the sentences were written with normal segmentation or as one connected string. Most of the four- and five-year-olds found the run-together versions perfectly acceptable, in fact better than the segmented ones. Those children who preferred segmented sentences broke them either into the number of nouns in the sentence (two) or into three parts: noun phrase, verb, noun phrase. Some found it very difficult to recognize three parts. One four-year-old girl asked the experimenter to rewrite the sentence, dividing it into three parts, but still she could not make sense of it. Finally she said, 'el oso . . . el oso come miel . . . ah, ya se! Hay dos osos, y la miel.' '(The bear . . . the bear eats honey . . . oh, I know! There are two bears and the honey.) Only one child, a six-year-old, divided the sentence into its words.

Working-class and middle-class children made the same types of responses, developmentally ordered as above. A child could be in one stage or simultaneously in one stage and either of those contiguous to it. Ferreiro suggests that the entire process is in accord with Piaget's theory of the acquisition of knowledge; a child must come to understand the writing system by reconstructing it for himself, that is, by 'reinventing' it (pp. 30-9).

Ferreiro (1980) reports a continuation of this line of study. For two years she monitored the development of thirty three- to six-year-olds from both nonliterate working-class families and highly literate middle-class families. She examined the children's spontaneous, unschooled writings. In an experiment similar to Lavine's (1977), Ferreiro asked the children to judge whether various strings of letters or numbers, singly and in combinations, could be read. The children's most important criteria appeared to be a minimum number of signs (three) and a variety of signs (p. 6).

Beyond those basic criteria, several others emerge at different times. The number of letters required may depend on some quantitative aspect of the referent(s). For example, an elephant requires more letters than a mouse, or plural nouns more than singular. A five-year-old produced the following example:

AOI	'gato'	(cat)
OIA	'gatito'	(little cat)
OAIOAIOAI	'gatitos'	(three little cats in the picture; he explains as he is writing: 'one little cat' (the first three letters); 'the little cats here' (six letters); 'another cat' (the three remaining letters))

Likewise, four-year-old Mariana required four letters to write her name (one for each year), seven letters to write her mother's two-syllable name, and 'as many as one thousand' to write her father's two-syllable name (p. 16).

At first, a child's writing can mean whatever he or she wishes. A given string of letters or words may represent any number of disparate messages, and several different texts may represent the same message. Gradually, similar messages come to require similar texts, even to the point of two phonetically distinct but semantically related words having to be written with similar letters. For instance, Ferreiro presented a four-year-old with the word GALLO (cock) and asked her to write 'gallina' (hen). The child said that since a hen is smaller than a cock, fewer letters are needed, so she wrote GALL. Being then asked to write 'pollito' (chick), she wrote GAL, because it is smaller still (p. 16).

All of the variations in written messages are accomplished within the requirements of minimum number and variety of letters, using the letters that the child knows at the time. The child discovers that letters can be combined and recombined to produce varied messages even before he learns that letters correspond to sounds (p. 8).

Ferreiro asserts that a child discovers syllabic spelling in the process of reconciling the notion of quantitative correspondence with the realization that even singular referents have more than one letter in their representations. The child begins to search for some principle of segmenting individual words, arriving at the idea of syllabic segmentation. In its earliest versions, this means that each letter corresponds to one syllable, so that 'gatito,' for instance, requires three letters. Conflict then arises between this correspondence and the minimum number requirement: 'gato,' having two syllables, should require two letters, but two letters are insufficient, so a third letter is added to make it a real word. This results in a contrast such as the following (p. 13):

Spelling:	O I A	A OI
Reading:	ga-ti-to	ga-to
English gloss:	little cat	cat

At this point, the child has begun to include elements in writing for purely formal reasons, but not in relationship to speech. Quantitative relations between the written word and its referent (rather than its spoken form) are still most important to him.

In further tests of the importance of quantitative considerations, Ferreiro displayed sentences which contained as many words as the number of objects referred to, such as *mama compro tres tacos* (mama bought three tacos). She found that children were very pleased to have the numbers coincide. They found 'mama' in one word and three tacos in the others. When Ferreiro removed one word from the written sentence, some children interpreted it to mean that mama bought just two tacos; with another word removed, she had bought only one.

Another criterion appeared with middle-class children (but not with lower-class children) in Geneva: only truthful utterances can be written down. Seventy per cent of the children between four and six years of age said that *la tortue vole* (the turtle flies) could not be written down. In fact, the truth of a written sentence seemed to be self-evident and of great importance to these children. One four-year-old, presented with 'un pajaro vuela' (a bird flies), said 'I already knew it. . . . Yes, because birds fly, then a bird flies.' When Ferreiro asked him to write 'There are no birds,' he replied that it could be done only with twisted letters, because it is false.

Ferreiro concludes that children construct a series of hypotheses before realizing that alphabetic writing is based on correspondences between sounds and spellings. It is in this sense that a child 'reinvents' the writing system in coming to understand it (pp. 19-24).

Together, the work of Clay, Lavine and Ferreiro has revealed rich development in children's early conceptions of writing. Even at age three, some children distinguish writing from pictures and then make further distinctions among kinds of written symbols.

During a period of about three years, they try out various hypotheses about the relation of written language to objects and then to spoken language.

Some of these attempts, such as syllabic writing, recapitulate aspects of the historical development of writing systems. By contrast, alphabetic spelling is a relatively late and sophisticated idea. Gleitman and Rozin (1977) argue for the same conclusion on two bases: a review of the history of writing, and experiments in teaching children who had had difficulty with alphabetic spelling to read a syllabary. Thus, what is distinctive about creative spellers is not only their spontaneity, but also their early mastery of this crucial concept which causes difficulty for many other children.

Children may begin formal training in literacy at any point in this largely hidden process. At that time, they receive instruction from parents and teachers who may scarcely be aware that there can be non-alphabetic writing systems; they are in no position to recognize some of the extraordinary hypotheses that children invent. There must often be a poor fit between what a child does and what an adult perceives or what learning materials present. Awaiting further research on these relations, we must now at least recognize that the real function of preschool and primary education is not to introduce children to written language but to help them refine the conceptions that they have already created of it.

B Segmentation

In addition to having some conception of the nature and purpose of writing and a notion of which words are represented, a would-be speller must be able to perform a specific analysis: he or she must be able to divide the stream of speech into the units which are represented by alphabetic spelling. Fundamentally, and especially for beginners, these units are phonemes – what we ordinarily think of as speech sounds.

Liberman, Liberman, Mattingly and Shankweiler (1980) review several studies of the development of this skill. They point out that this segmentation is problematic, both in theory and in practice. In theory, it is not obvious how speech can be segmented, for physically it is more like a stream than like a row of buckets. What we think of as discrete sounds actually flow together, overlap and influence each other substantially. This has been an essential problem in phonological analysis for more than fifty years, and it is still not entirely clear in what sense speech consists of discrete units, or why it can be so perceived.

In practice, this segmentation is difficult for some children and constitutes a major obstacle to learning to read and write, according to Liberman *et al.* Phonemic segmentation is necessary for speaking Pig Latin and for making up rhymes or alliteration, but reading and writing are the only central linguistic skills which depend on it. For everyday speaking and listening, language *could* be made up of unanalyzable words or syllables.

Liberman, Shankweiler, Fischer and Carter (1974) tested the segmentation skills of children in nursery school, kindergarten and first grade. They compared the difficulty of counting phonemes with that of counting syllables, using matched groups of children at each age. The experimenter spoke a word, which a child repeated, and then the child was to tap a wooden dowel on a table, once for each syllable or phoneme in the word.

At every grade level, children counted syllables more accurately then phonemes. None of the nursery school children and only 17 per cent of the kindergarteners could count phonemes, compared with 46 per cent and 48 per cent, respectively, who could count syllables. By contrast, 70 per cent of the first graders could count phonemes, although even more (90 per cent) could count syllables. Treiman and Baron (1981) show that this ability to count segments is associated with one aspect of reading skill, namely using spelling-sound correspondences.

Liberman *et al.* attribute the much greater success of first graders in phoneme-counting to reading instruction, rather than to cognitive maturation alone. Citing the poor segmentation performance of illiterate adults in Portugal, compared to a control group of literate adults (Morais, Cary, Alegria and Bertelson, 1979), Liberman *et al.* conclude that linguistic awareness depends upon, or evolves with, reading instruction.

Bradley and Bryant (1978) distinguished cause from effect in the relation between segmenting and learning to read and spell. By eliciting judgments of rhyme and alliteration, they compared the segmentation skills of normal and 'backward' readers and spellers. Both groups had the reading and spelling skills of seven-year-olds; the normal children were about seven years old, while the 'backward' ones were about ten-and-a-half. Both groups were of normal intelligence for their age. Despite their greater maturity, the backward readers were much poorer at judging sounds. This deficit could not have been due to a difference in reading/spelling performance because there was none. More likely, Bradley and Bryant reasoned, the 'backward' children had trouble with alphabetic spelling because they were poor at segmenting speech.

Zifcak (1977) studied the relationships among three measures of first graders' phonological awareness: spelling words containing nasals, segmenting words into phonemes, and eliding syllables and phonemes from words. The subjects were first asked to spell a dictated list of words containing nasals in various positions. In a pilot study, eleven children had omitted nasals before voiceless stops in 57 per cent of their spellings, while they represented 99 per cent of the nasals in other positions. This result thus replicated Read's (1971) observations of creative spelling (see pp. 11-14).

The main study was conducted with first graders in a socioeconomically and racially mixed school in Rhode Island. The children were first given a spelling test with words containing nasals in various positions: before voiceless or voiced homorganic stops, e.g., *rink* and *land*, before non-homorganic stops, e.g., *hummed*, and in other positions, e.g., *name* and *ton*. Read's 'pointer' test (see pp. 14-17) was then administered to those children who consistently represented or consistently did not represent the preconsonantal nasals.

Next, the children performed a phoneme or syllable segmentation task. They were asked to listen to a spoken word, repeat it, and then tap with a plastic hammer, once for each segment (phoneme or syllable) in the word. This was followed by a phonological elision task, in which the child was asked to say a word and then to repeat it, omitting one syllable or phoneme.

The results on the nasals tests again replicated Read's. The children represented a separate nasal segment before voiceless stops in only 35 per cent of their spellings but represented 99 per cent of nasals in other positions. On the 'pointer' task, all of the children who pointed to the vowel as the location of the nasal sound had failed to represent a nasal in the initial spelling test. Zifcak concurs with Read's interpretation that these are phonetic judgments categorizing nasality with the preceding vowel. All of the children who pointed to the space between the vowel and the final stop had represented a nasal in that position in spelling.

Zifcak found significant correlations (p < .01) among the three measures of phonological awareness, of which the largest was between spelling and phoneme segmentation (r = .74) (p. 44). In a stepwise multiple regression, phoneme segmentation ability contributed most to the prediction of reading success (R = .78, p < .01). Invented spelling scores improved the prediction slightly, and no other variable (phonological elision ability, intelligence, sex, age, or socioeconomic status of parents) contributed significantly (p. 51). Zifcak concludes that first graders must develop specific phonological knowledge before they can become skilled readers.

In the work of Liberman and her colleagues, and elsewhere, phonemic segmentation has been said to require one form of linguistic awareness, that is, conscious knowledge of the structure of language as opposed to the unconscious manipulation which is involved in all use of language. In one sense this claim may seem misleading, because any child who can spell novel words must be able to segment them, and as we have seen, some quite young children are able to spell but give little indication of conscious analysis. On the other hand, young children can also correct themselves and occasionally create linguistic jokes such as puns, both of which require some attention to the form of language. (For further examples, see Sinclair, Jarvella and Levelt (1978), especially the papers by Slobin and Clark.)

Moreover, phonemic segmentation resembles other skills requiring linguistic analysis in that it is acquired after initial language acquisition, it usually requires explicit instruction, and people vary considerably in the ease with which they can do it. Gleitman and Gleitman (1970) offer striking examples of this property of metalinguistic skills. So long as we recognize that analytic use of language may involve widely varying degrees of actual awareness, we are quite justified in regarding phonemic segmentation as one such analytic skill.

Clearly, the research on segmentation supports and helps to explain the observation that learning to spell alphabetically is a relatively late development. Not only does it depend upon the concept that writing represents spoken language, as opposed to objects, and that it represents speech sounds in particular, but it also requires the specific skill of phonemic segmentation, which is difficult for at least some children.

What we may never have are reliable comparisons of natural development across various kinds of writing systems: alphabetic, syllabic and logographic. As noted in Chapter 4, comparative studies are few in number and rather primitive. There are not many logographic writing systems and even fewer syllabic ones; Japanese, the principal modern example of the latter, actually makes use of all three types. Moreover, implicit or explicit comparisons with English will always be inconclusive because its orthography represents multiple levels and contains many spellings that are not predictable on *any* basis. Nevertheless, it is clear that alphabetic spelling has some difficult prerequisites.

It by no means follows that alphabetic writing is undesirable; it may be far easier than other systems to use and even to learn, given an initial grasp of what it represents. A syllabary for English, with its thousands of different syllables, would be far more difficult to learn than the syllabaries for Japanese, which has fewer than eighty types. What the research reviewed above does imply is that we must give more attention to how children learn the nature of alphabetic writing: what prior concepts are required, how we can recognize readiness, what teaching techniques are effective, and why some children have far more difficulty than others.

We can now proceed from the cognitive prerequisites for spelling to some developments that occur alongside it, in general cognition and in reading.

C Spelling and Piaget's theory of cognitive development

One line of research has sought to correlate stages of spelling acquisition with the stages of cognitive growth described by Jean Piaget. These studies have assumed that most children develop through a sequence of spelling strategies, from the so-called letter-name strategy to abstract, nearly standard, spelling, and that this development normally occurs between kindergarten and the late elementary-school years. (See Chapter 2.) Piaget and his colleagues have shown that during approximately the same period, children progress from preoperational to concrete operational thought. Zutell (1975, 1980) and Beers (1980) examined the relation between these parallel stages of spelling acquisition and cognitive development.

Do spelling strategies actually draw upon the general-purpose and rather abstract mental abilities that define Piagetian stages? Elkind (1974, as cited by Beers, 1980, p. 74) suggests that in order to spell, a child must distinguish various properties of a letter, e.g., its name from the sounds that it represents. Such distinctions are characteristic of the stage of cognitive development known as concrete operations. Thus reliance on the letter-name strategy in spelling may indicate preoperational thought.

Zutell (1975, 1980) set out to measure the correlation between children's spelling abilities and their performance on Piagetian 'conservation' tasks, which distinguish between preoperational and concrete operational thought. Zutell proposed four hypotheses:

- that the quality of children's spelling improves as their grade level increases;
- that children's spelling strategies become less sophisticated with more complex words;
- that there is an interaction between grade level and word complexity; and
- that there is a significant correlation between spelling strategies and cognitive functions, as measured by Piagetian decentration tasks.

Zutell examined the spelling of five features: short vowels, long vowels, past tenses, doubled consonants and derivational pairs such as inflame/inflammation. Two spelling lists of eighteen words each, including a total of six low-frequency words from each of the above five categories, were given to sixty children, fifteen in each grade from one to four. Each child was also given a battery of Piagetian conservation tasks.

Zutell rated the children's spellings on a scale based on Beers (1974), with two additional categories. From least to most mature, they were:

- no sound-letter matches at all,
- vowel omitted,
- letter-name spelling,
- transitional spelling,
- correct spelling of feature studied, but in an incorrectly spelled word,
- standard spelling.

Zutell found significant effects of grade-level and the predicted interaction with complexity. The children used more mature spelling strategies at higher grade levels, but less mature ones with more complex words.

Surprisingly, however, the second graders used less mature strategies than the first graders. Zutell had expected the 'transitional' spelling strategies to appear mainly in second-grade spellings, but these second graders used primarily the letter-name strategy. (Their teacher reported that that class was less advanced than average.) The third graders were already beyond the transitional strategy, so Zutell did not observe them.

From easiest to most difficult, the spelling features were: short and long vowels, past tenses and doubled consonants, and derivationally-related pairs. The difficulty of this last group agrees with Marino's finding about morphophonemically complex words.

Factor analysis revealed two distinct factors, one for spelling categories and one for decentration tasks. These two factors were significantly correlated (r = .56), even with the effect of grade level controlled (r = .36), p < .01 for both correlations. The period of transition from preoperational to concrete operational thinking was parallel to that from the letter-name strategy to higher spelling strategies. Zutell concludes that the cognitive skills required for more abstract spelling are like those measured by the conservation tasks.

Beers (1980) sought to fill the gap at second grade left by Zutell's study. Expecting second graders to display transitional spelling most clearly, she tested 116 of them with spelling dictations, six conservation tasks, and a standard test of reading comprehension and vocabulary.

Total conservation score correlated significantly with age, reading comprehension and vocabulary. However, it correlated significantly with only one of the six spelling categories, that of 'short *i*' (/I/). Even in that case, r = .33, so that these two measures have only about 11 per cent of their variance in common. (The spelling of 'short *a*' (/æ/) was significantly correlated with two of the six conservation tasks, but not with the total.) Beers argues that it makes sense for the short vowels to be related to conservation, because for them the (immature) letter-name strategy does not yield standard spellings, but there is no apparent explanation for the differences among the three short vowels tested.

The studies by Zutell and Beers have certainly shown that development in spelling occurs alongside the transition from preoperational to concrete operational thought. But the degree to which one is predictable from the other is only moderate, and some positive correlation was to be expected in any case, considering that the two sequences occur during approximately the same years, and that each includes only a few stages and generally proceeds in only one direction.

Is there a deeper relation? Is the attainment of concrete operational thinking a prerequisite for more abstract spelling, for example? Measures of correlation cannot reach this question. To answer it, we need longitudinal studies or the opportunity to control one of the variables. The most that one can say now is that there is a plausible connection between more abstract thinking and more abstract spelling, and that the two have been shown to be significantly correlated. In any case, cognitive skills other than those measured by conservation tasks must certainly affect spelling development, including metacognition, sequencing and memory.

In addition, we need to define the stages of spelling development in terms of processes. In particular, the stage now known as 'transitional' and defined in relation to standard spelling must be reanalyzed in terms of what the speller is attempting to represent and how, as the 'letter-name' strategy is now defined. Even standard spelling, or approximations to standard spelling at the first-grade level, must be analyzed in terms of spelling processes. Such an analysis must take account of not only phonological development but also effects of reading experience and spelling instruction, which become increasingly important.

Future studies may also benefit from revised conceptions of cognitive development. Piaget assumed that it results from the interaction of human biological dispositions with the sociocultural environment. His model, with its series of rather independent stages, may not do justice to such an interaction; it fits the biological foundations better than the environmental influences, including schooling.

Newer models based on Piaget's have tried to correct this weakness. They hypothesize fewer absolute stages, with more substages and more emphasis on transitions and on individual variation, a major factor in spelling. The periods of transition are considered to be the times when environmental factors are most significant, i.e., when biological dispositions are realized under the influence of environmental factors. In the case of spelling, these factors are likely to involve instruction and the reading/writing experience of the child. Fischer (1980) elaborates a general model of this sort, not yet applied to spelling.

D Spelling and reading

There is clearly some relation between spelling and reading. The two have complementary functions based on the same writing sytem, and children learn both skills within approximately the same period. Anecdotal evidence suggests that reading experience influences spelling proficiency, and for the most part, we can read and write the same words. As Paul Bissex observed at age five, 'Once you know how to spell something, you know how to read it!' (Bissex, 1980, p. 122).

However, we also know that at the margins our performance of the two skills is not the same. All of us occasionally find ourselves unable to spell a word which we could read without difficulty. For many adults and almost all children, this is an everyday experience. This fact alone makes us wonder how similar the two processes really are.

Frith (1980) studied the spelling and reading processes of 'unexpectedly poor spellers': twelve-year-olds who were good readers but poor spellers. She showed first that these children's spelling errors are different from those of children who are poor spellers *and* poor readers: about two-thirds of the errors of the former group are phonetically reasonable; fewer than half of the errors of the latter group are. (Frith uses 'phonetic' in a non-technical sense that does not include most of the spellings discussed in Chapter One.) Next Frith showed that the good readers/poor spellers also read differently from children who were good at both reading and spelling. Specifically, the former were poorer at reading aloud or at reading nonsense words; that is, they were poorer at producing the sound, as opposed to the meaning, of what they read. Finally, with a variety of tasks, Frith showed that the good readers/poor spellers probably read 'by partial cues;' that is, they did not typically attend to the spelling of the words they read, but relied more heavily on context, shape and some of the letters in a target word. Frith suggests that this strategy may yield faster reading but less detailed knowledge of English spelling. The good readers/poor spellers could produce phonetically plausible spellings, but did not know which pattern was appropriate to which word.

As Bryant and Bradley (1980) note, the commonplace evidence that spelling is more difficult than reading is ambiguous: it may indicate a difference in processes, or it may be merely additional proof that producing language is more difficult than receiving it. More telling would be evidence of the reverse: cases in which reading is more difficult than spelling. They discovered precisely such cases by asking children to read and spell the same words on different occasions. The sample was nearly the same as in Bradley and Bryant's (1978) study of segmentation: all of the children had a 'reading age' of about seven-and-a-half years, but some of them were normal readers (about seven years old), while the others were poor readers (about ten-and-a-half years old).

Most children in both groups spelled at least one word correctly that they failed to read correctly, and many of them spelled more words correctly than they read correctly. However, the words most frequently read but not spelled were 'irregular,' such as *school* and *light*, while those most frequently spelled but not read were 'regular,' such as *bun* and *mat*. For this and other reasons, Bryant and Bradley suggested that children at an early stage of reading development use different strategies in reading and spelling: they 'depend on visual chunks when they read and phonological segments when they spell.' This distinction is characteristic of only the beginning stages, however; even children just a bit older than seven could read almost all the words they could spell on average. Bryant and Bradley hypothesize that most children quickly learn to use both strategies in both processes, but that Frith's unexpectedly poor spellers are the exception.

Nowhere is the initial separation between spelling and reading more evident than with creative spellers. It is typical for them to be able to read words in standard spelling and yet to spell those same words in their own nonstandard way (Read, 1981). This apparent paradox occurs even with words that they have read many times. When creative spellers are confronted with the contrast between their spelling and the standard form which they can read, they typically see nothing wrong with either (Read, 1975, pp. 93, 109);

they simply do not assume that the two must be alike.

Gerritz (1974, pp. 63-7) also notes the separation between reading instruction and spelling for her first graders. Their reading series introduced the standard spellings for vowels in a controlled manner (spelling of [I] and [æ] in Book One, of [ɛ] in Book Two and so on), so Gerritz was able to observe the relation between this instruction and the appearance of the same spellings in the children's spontaneous writing. Except for those spellings that were introduced *before* half of the children had begun to spell at all, the spellings introduced in the reading series appeared to have no direct effect on the children's own writing. In forty-six of forty-nine cases in which a child was using a nonstandard spelling when a corresponding standard one was introduced in the reading lessons, the child did not change his or her spelling. In the remaining three cases, the time between the teaching of a spelling and the appearance of that spelling in the child's own writing ranged from one to two-and-a-half months.

All of these observations indicate that spelling and reading performance differs for young children, and that for some children this difference persists. The performance differs because the processes differ; the circumstantial similarities between the two are misleading. One difference is that young children continue to spell sound-by-sound long after they stop reading familiar words in this manner. Reading experience does influence spelling performance (and vice-versa); in fact, Frith (1980) suggests that specific reading strategies lead to better spelling. But because the processes differ, the influence cannot be direct or immediate.

Is this simply another case (like the development of spoken language) in which receptive skills outrun productive ones temporarily, or do the processes remain distinct even in adulthood, when the gap in performance is no longer so obvious? Certainly reading and spelling strategies both become more varied and flexible; in that sense, they become more similar. However, the way in which they diversify is not the same. Marsh, Friedman, Welch and Desberg (1980) point out that a young reader facing an unknown word often substitutes a known word that fits the syntactic and semantic context, whereas a speller has no really similar strategy. Basically, the reader learns to use the wider context, while the speller learns to use conditional regularities and morphophonemic consistency. Syntactic and semantic context are essential to reading but irrelevant to spelling, except in distinguishing between homophones or in choosing which word to spell. For that reason, we must suppose that reading and spelling processes continue to differ even in maturity, and certainly they differ from one individual to another. As research attends to processes rather than merely correctness, we can look for more insight into these differences.

II A conception of spelling development

The studies reviewed in this chapter do not provide a sufficient basis for inferring a precise developmental sequence. Comparing and integrating these studies is difficult because most were conducted without reference to the others, and they sampled different populations using different tasks. Even studies like Ferreiro's, which give evidence of a developmental sequence, are necessarily cautious about making really precise claims. However, these studies, together with the observations of creative spelling and studies of subsequent development, do provide a basis for an outline of spelling development. In this section, we will try to knit these studies into a coherent shape, albeit vague at some points and certainly incomplete.

Development toward spelling must begin with distinguishing writing from other activities in both form and function. At a very early stage, children perceive that writing represents something, as opposed to being purely formal; it is not just decorative, for example. That children grasp the representational nature of writing so quickly testifies to the fundamental place of representation in the schema through which they interpret their world. Being read to must help a child recognize the nature of writing. Creating a story populated with characters and events from no material other than paper must be highly salient; a child quickly infers that the marks on the paper play some role in this entertaining process.

However, even if reading is a clue to the representational nature of writing, it by no means follows that writing and reading are directly related in detail, that every word read must have been written down, for example, and children do not draw that inference until much later. Rather, they believe at first that writing represents objects rather than corresponding to language at all, and they expect to find resemblances in size or quantity between the object and its written representation, just as in pictorial representation.

At about the same time, children begin to identify the form of writing, distinguishing Roman letters from other non-pictorial symbols. Also at this early stage, they begin to infer that writing is linear, although the direction that prevails in the local writing system remains outside their grasp for some months or years. Directionality may come later because it depends on neurological changes, as is often suggested, or because the characters and their linear arrangement can be seen in the text itself, whereas the direction must be observed in writing and reading *processes*.

In moving toward actual spelling, the next major step is the recognition that writing represents not objects but spoken language, i.e., that at least some parts of a spoken sentence are written down. Whatever the writing system, a child cannot proceed without this recognition. Ferreiro's work suggests that this insight arises only gradually, however obvious it may seem (to adults) to leap to the conclusion that all words are to be represented. Children recognize progressively more abstract parts of sentences, it seems. Certainly the dawn of linguistic awareness plays a role here: the gradual and still largely unconscious recognition that there *are* linguistic objects in addition to concrete ones.

Near the end of this development, children may be ready for a purely formal but non-alphabetic writing system, such as a syllabary. That is, they are ready to represent all linguistic units of some type larger than a single phonological segment.

Significantly, children do not attempt to represent *all* of the recognizable linguistic units. For example, little or no allophonic variation is represented in creative spelling, although allophonic variation *influences* it, as in the omission of nasals in their preconsonantal forms. Similarly, we have no reports of children trying to represent intonation, except in more-or-less standard and indirect ways, such as boldface print and exclamation points. In these two omissions, children's spelling resembles most standard writing systems, which ignore not only allophonic variation, but also tone and intonation, even in tone languages. A major task for research is to explain how children manage to infer that alphabetic spelling represents phonemes (more-or-less), but not their allophonic variation nor the prosodic matrix in which the phonemes are realized. To say that children try to represent just what they perceive as meaningful or salient cannot account for overlooking prosodic structure, since tone, intonation, stress and duration can all be semantically significant.

The next major development is truly a crux: the recognition that spelling represents speech sounds, and the ability to identify those speech sounds as if they were discrete entities. Liberman *et al.* (1980) and Treiman and Baron (1981) have focussed on the latter issue, but otherwise, research to date has not systematically distinguished these two separable developments. As we have seen, some children have great difficulty in taking these steps, and it seems altogether likely that some adult illiterates' disabilities begin at this point. Morais *et al.* (1979) indicate that these developments are not likely to take place in the absence of explicit instruction; Read, Zhang, Nie and Ding (forthcoming) shows that they are specific to alphabetic writing.

It is therefore significant that creative spellers are able to segment speech at an early age without explicit instruction, on the basis of examples of reading and spelling in their home and preschool environments. Letter-names and toys with movable letters may be useful tools, but they do not solve the segmentation problem. How perception and cognition interact in this process, and how unconscious and conscious knowledge (including explicit learning) are related, are key questions which have yet to be answered. At any rate, a child who has solved this problem, who is sufficiently independent, and who has examples of spelling and the necessary opportunity, has all the prerequisites for creative spelling.

As we have seen, children's spelling at this stage is highly phonetic in the sense that the segmentation and classification of speech sounds takes account of their phonetic structure. The process of spelling is also sound-by-sound; several observers have noted that children 'sound out' individual speech sounds (or clusters) as they spell, and their questions at this stage typically have to do with the spelling of individual sounds (Bissex, 1980, p. 190). In this respect, spelling contrasts with reading, which at an early stage begins to focus on the word level, although children 'sound out' words which they cannot identify in context. Moreover, many children evidently conceive of the two activities as being separate; most creative spellers are not concerned that their spelling differs from the standard form, which they can read.

Not surprisingly, however, a child's spelling is soon affected by his growing acquaintance with the standard variety. What the Virginia researchers have called 'transitional' spelling is simply new standard forms alongside old nonstandard ones. Some of these influences are easy to identify; they are standard spellings in the wrong positions or the wrong words. As Gerritz and others have observed, though, such influences are spotty and often slow to appear, apparently because reading and spelling processes are basically different.

Marsh *et al.* (1980) outline the development of spelling strategies from this point on in a way which fits neatly with the evidence from other studies. They show that sequential encoding of phonemes continues to improve beyond grade two, but that it reaches a ceiling by grade five. During those same years, children learn to make greater use of spelling regularities which are conditional upon context. The two cases studied by Marsh *et al.* are the use of CVC*e* (as in *race*) to represent a 'long' vowel and the use of *c* to represent /k/ before the letters *a, o* and *u*. Because spellings such as these show an increasing attention to orthographic context, they indicate the developing similarity between reading and spelling processes.

Marsh *et al.* also studied the development of 'analogical' spellings, such as JATION for a nonce word rhyming with *nation*. Nonce words were also presented in pairs intended to motivate morphophonemic or lexical spellings, such as CUSCLE/ CUSCULAR. Such spellings increased from second grade to fifth grade to college, but they were always in the minority: fifth graders produced analogical spellings for only 10 per cent of the pairs and 33 per cent of the individual words. Even college students produced only 24 per cent and 50 per cent, respectively. Marsh *et al.* account for this outcome in terms of the infrequency of the words which were expected to motivate the analogical spellings, such as *muscle-muscular*. Frequency might also account for the greater number of analogical spellings for individual words, since at least the examples cited by Marsh *et al.* are relatively frequent words (*nation, soldier* and *length*), in which only the first sound was changed. Another factor may have been the lack of any meaning relation in the nonce pairs, unlike the relations in real pairs such as *muscle/muscular*. Recall, however, that Zutell (1975) and Marino

(1978) found that lexical spellings for real words develop late. In reading, on the other hand, analogical strategies develop somewhat earlier (Marsh, Friedman, Welch and Desberg, 1981).

In summary, then, phoneme-by-phoneme encoding is the major spelling strategy in both the primary and the early elementary years, but after the first or second grade, the phonetic representations found in creative spelling give way to a reliance on frequent correspondences in standard spelling. This process occurs at about the same time as, and may be dependent on, the attainment of concrete operations in general cognition. At first, it yields spellings in which the two bases are mixed. Also during the elementary years, children make rapidly increasing use of conditional spelling rules, reaching a ceiling for at least some of these by the fifth grade. The morphophonemic spellings which are characteristic of part of the English lexicon, especially polysyllabic Romance words like *divine-divinity*, begin to appear during these years, but are not yet productive. For some spellers, they may not become productive even in adulthood.

Reading uses similar strategies, especially the recognition of conditional correspondences and morphophonemic ('analogical') spellings, but these develop more rapidly than their counterparts in spelling. In fact, there may never be a stage in reading at which children rely as exclusively on spellings of individual sounds, regardless of context, as they do in beginning spelling. At this point, it seems doubtful that reading and spelling ever become really parallel, mainly because syntactic and semantic structure are much more relevant to reading.

A For parents and teachers

We assume that parents and teachers reading this section share a basic goal: to encourage the development of a child's writing, including her beginning spelling. With this encouragement, the child may acquire some skills earlier than she otherwise would have, but that is not our aim; the child is not competing with herself or with others. The great need is for her to enjoy writing, to use it as a tool in play and in learning other skills, and in the end to realize her full potential as a writer.

How well a parent or teacher (let us call them both 'teacher') achieves this goal seems to depend more on attitudes than on techniques or materials. Fundamental is the belief that an interest in writing is natural, just like an interest in art; every child enjoys playing with both kinds of representation. Equally important is an adult's genuine interest in the child's writing; the only external reward the child wants or needs is for an adult to appreciate both the message in her writing and its form. Finally, one effective manifestation of a teacher's attitude toward writing is what he does with it himself. Although children develop writing skills in all sorts of homes and schools, it is easiest when their adult models enjoy writing and use it for a purpose that they value. If, on the other hand, the teacher feels that writing is laborious or fears the 'bad spelling habits' that a child seems to be acquiring, his responses will convey those reservations from the beginning.

Teachers must also recognize certain characteristics of development – for example, that it comes in fits and starts; a child may make obvious progress in one month and none in the next. Interest, too, comes and goes; a child may devote hours to writing at one period and then do no more for months. Another part of a healthy attitude is recognizing that there are large individual differences in the development of writing, just as there are in other skills. What is for one child a period of rapid growth may be for another a period of apparent stagnation. Likewise, there are considerable differences in the end result. What one child masters readily may remain an obstacle to another; large unexplained differences in spelling facility are commonplace.

In one sense, the importance of attitudes is good news for parents and teachers. It means that children can develop well in all sorts of circumstances; both Maria Montessori and Emilia Ferreiro have portrayed the growth of writing in severely disadvantaged surroundings. It also means that no temporary lapse by a teacher will seriously hinder a child's growth. The urge to put messages into writing is strong enough that it will not be extinguished in a moment of neglect or impatience.

But in other ways, the importance of attitudes is bad news: it means that a favorable environment cannot merely be purchased from a catalog of learning materials or imposed by a curriculum committee. We cannot feign or impose a positive attitude toward writing. If we do not value a child's accomplishments, peculiar as they sometimes appear, or if we do not really believe that writing can be both enjoyable and useful, a child who is with us many hours each day is sure to sense how we really feel and will almost certainly grow to share our feelings.

Given positive attitudes toward writing in general and toward children's writing in particular, what can a teacher do to foster development? For a start, he can lay a foundation early; children's writing begins with being read to and with observing parents engaged in reading and writing. He can be alert for certain landmarks: the first linear scribbles, the first Roman letters, the first representation of speech segments, the first creative spellings, the appearance of standard correspondences, and the first spellings that do *not* represent speech sounds but are abstract, like standard spelling. Bissex (1980) noted a change in the nature of her son's questions: from asking how to spell a sound to asking how to spell a word. Recognizing these landmarks assures the teacher that the child is making progress, even when most of the spelling is not yet standard. With this recognition, the teacher will be excited, and the child will sense that enthusiasm.

When the spelling begins to represent speech sounds, the teacher can listen to the sounds that the spelling represents. Then he is more likely to recognize some phonetic bases (even without specific training), and his response to the writing and to the child's questions will be informed by this recognition. Whether or not a teacher corrects a child's spelling, merely saying, 'I can hear why you spelled it that way' says a great deal about the value and the reasonableness of the child's own efforts.

Physical equipment is easily provided. A movable alphabet (toy blocks, cards or small pieces of wood with letters) can make life easier for a child who wants to spell but who cannot yet manipulate a crayon or pencil. Later, ordinary paper and writing implements may be sufficient, although some children like to use a typewriter or computer.

Like adult writers, children sometimes need a little peace and even solitude. Among those who have written the most are only children with busy parents and children who have been mildly ill for a time. Even though children are amazingly adaptable, a little space for writing is also useful, especially in a classroom.

Providing the mental equipment requires mainly example and enthusiasm, but also includes answering the child's questions, which may be frequent. Children who write the most are those who have much to write *about*; some of this background comes from being read to, as well as from varied experiences at home and in school.

In general, the teacher's role is to facilitate, rather than to direct. Writing is part of a child's play with language, especially in the beginning, and the specific activities must grow out of a child's interests. Whether she is writing a note, a poem, an invitation, a prayer, a story, a caption, or directions, she is likely to direct herself rather than to march to an adult drummer.

A teacher's strongest reservations about encouraging independent spelling may be the fear that immature spellings will persist, that the child will learn bad habits. In fact, nonstandard spellings do often persist, as Gerritz noted in comparing her first graders' reading and spelling. But Gerritz noticed something more. In her classroom, where children were encouraged to write, the reading workbooks gave a different kind of spelling practice, so she observed the relation between the spontaneous and the guided spelling. There was little relation:

> the children clearly did not transfer what they had learned to read, and had written many times in their reading program, to what they were writing on their own. . . . Despite the children's having filled in missing vowel after missing vowel in their programmed readers, they did not carry the spellings over into their own writing. (p. 66)

If the independent spellers in Gerritz's class persisted in their nonstandard ways, did their spelling and writing suffer in the long run? On a test of recognizing correct spellings at the beginning of grade two, some of Gerritz's pupils performed less well than children from other classes, who had not been encouraged to spell on their own, but by the beginning of grade three, there was no longer a difference. Gerritz adds,

> Second grade teachers did not comment on the poor quality of the first grade writers' conventional spelling, but on the ease and eagerness with which they wrote; on actual spelling tasks, in contrast to [the test], the children who participated in the study apparently did not carry any more bad habits with them to grade two than did the other children in the school. (p. 99)

How can a teacher learn productive attitudes and useful techniques for facilitating a child's spelling? Most effective is observation; seeing what can be done with writing in a lively preschool classroom is convincing. But books can be helpful; Ferreiro and Teberosky (1982) describe children's early concepts of writing; Temple, Nathan and Burris (1982) describe writing development through the elementary school years; and Bissex (1980) recounts one child's development in writing and reading up to age ten, from a mother's and researcher's point of view. Carol Chomsky (1971, 1975a and b) gives an account of children's creative spelling and describes how some teachers have encouraged writing in first grade; Fox and Allen (1983) provide an integrated approach to teaching language arts, including a conception of writing development and ideas for promoting it. Clay (1975) and Montessori (1964) provide additional background.

Appendix I
Phonetic transcriptions used in this book (Example words as pronounced in North Central United States)

Vowels		Consonants	
i	beat	p	pop
I	bit	b	bib
e	bait	t	tot
ɛ	bet	d	did
æ	bat	k	kick
ɑ	father	g	gag
ɔ	bought	m	mime
o	boat	n	nine
ʋ	put	ŋ	sing
u	boot	f	fife
ə	about, sofa	v	vine
ʌ	putt	θ	thin
aI	bite	ð	then
aʋ	bout	s	sis
ɔI	boy	z	zip
ɚ	bird, father	š	ship
		ž	measure
Semi-vowels		h	heat
j	yet	r	red
w	wet	l	lull
		č	cheap
		ǰ	jeep

Appendix II
Examples of young children's spellings

1 Boy, age 4:

TUOS.DAY.NIT.I.WIS.PLAYIG.WITH.LORA.
Tuesday night I was playing with Laura,
AND.I.MARED.LORA.WINTS.I.GIT.AGRE.
and I married Laura. Once I got angry
AND.I.FIDI.WITH.HIR.AND.I.LAFFT.IN.
and I fighted with her, and I left in
TO.THE.CCHIN.THAN.AFTR.I.WIL.I.I.
to the kitchen. Then after a while I
MARED.HIR.I.GAN.
married her again.

2 Same boy, age 4:

HOW R YOU WAN YOU GAD I CHANS
How are you? When you get a chance,
SAND IS OL I LADR
send us all a letter.
RAD R YOU TACEG CAR IV
Red, are you taking care of
YORSALF
yourself?

3 Same boy, age 5:

DEAR – SALMA I . LIKE YOUR . LATR . I . AM . NAT .
Dear Selma, I like your letter. I am not
FILG . WALE . I . HAV . A . SORE . THROT . BUT .
feeling well. I have a sore throat, but

AM . DOEG . PRETE . WAL . MY . MOM . AND . DAD . IR . OL
am doing pretty well. My Mom and Dad are all
RITE . I   ENJOY . COLAKTGE . STMP STAMP STAMP
right. I enjoy collecting stamps.
I . DO . THEKCE . THTE . ITSE . FUN DO . YOU . KOLACT
I do think that it's fun. Do you collect
STMPS BCOZ . IF . YOU . DO . I . WEL . SAND . YOU . SAME .
stamps, because if you do, I will send you some
GUDE . STMPS . I . KANE . HRDLE . TOKE . I . HAV .
good stamps. I can hardly talk. I have
TO . STAE . IN . BAD . I . DRENK TEA . AND . SIK . COF .
to stay in bed. I drink tea and suck cough
DRPS. I . RILE . WEDE . LIKE . TO . SEE . YOU . VARE . MUCH .
drops. I really would like to see you very much.
I . AM . WALANF . TO . RITE YOU . THES . LATRE . MY
I am well enough to write you this letter. My
STMP . ABULBM . GEVS . DESKRIPSINOF ECHECANTRE.
stamp album gives descriptions of each country.

4 Girl, age 5:

HOO LICS HANE! HOO LICS HANE WAS OV PONA TIM
Who likes honey? Who likes honey? Once upon a time
THER WAS OV BER HOO LOVED HANE THE EAD
there was a bear who loved honey. The End.

5 Boy, age 4 years, 9 months:

THAY BROT MY TETH AND THAY POT A FILEN IN
They brushed my teeth, and they put a filling in.
THEY HAD A SPETHOL DRIL IT IS FOR TACIN OUT CABDES
They had a special drill; it is for taking out cavities.

6 Same boy, age 5 years, 4 months:

BLUE BERE PIE
Blueberry Pie
FIRST A PAWD OF BLUEBERES. THAN AD SOME GIGRBRED
First a pound of blueberries. Then add some gingerbead.
THAN BAC IT FOR 10 SEKIS.
Then bake it for 10 seconds.
CAK
Cake
FRST 4 CUPS OF SHGR. TEN AD 2 CUPS OF BUTTR
First 4 cups of sugar. Then add 2 cups of butter.

THAN AD SOME FRASTING.
Then add some frosting.
KUKES
Cookies
FRST AD GIGR BED. THAN PUT IN 5 CUPS OF
First add gingerbread. Then put in 5 cups of
CHAKLIT CHIP
chocolate chips.

7 Same boy, age 5:

DOT MAK NOYS
Don't make noise.
MY DADAAY WRX HIR
My Daddy works here.
THIS SI WER MI DADAAA WRX
This is where my Daddy works.
B CWIYIT
Be quiet.

Examples 2, 4 and 7 appeared in Read (1980). Used by permission of the editors.

Examples 5 and 6 appeared in Read (1981). Used by permission of Lawrence Erlbaum Associates, Inc.

Appendix III
Frequencies of spellings

The following tables present the frequencies and percentages of all spellings of selected phonemes in the corpus reported in Read (1975).

TABLE 1 *Phoneme: /ε/*

Age: Spelling	Under 6		Unknown		6 or over		All	
	Freq	Pct	Freq	Pct	Freq	Pct	Freq	Pct
a	96	49.7	32	34.0	63	38.7	191	42.4
e	72	37.3	40	42.6	80	49.1	192	42.7
i	11	5.7	6	6.4	8	4.9	25	5.6
(omit)	9	4.7	10	10.6	5	3.1	24	5.3
ee	2	1.0	2	2.1	1	0.6	5	1.1
ae	1	0.5	0	0.0	0	0.0	1	0.2
ai	1	0.5	0	0.0	0	0.0	1	0.2
fu	1	0.5	0	0.0	0	0.0	1	0.2
o	0	0.0	0	0.0	1	0.6	1	0.2
u	0	0.0	1	1.1	1	0.6	2	0.4
ei	0	0.0	1	1.1	0	0.0	1	0.2
ey	0	0.0	0	0.0	2	1.2	2	0.4
ea	0	0.0	1	1.1	2	1.2	3	0.7
ear	0	0.0	1	1.1	0	0.0	1	0.2
Totals	193	100.0	94	100.0	163	100.0	450	100.0

TABLE 2 *Phoneme: /I/*

Age: Spelling	Under 6		Unknown		6 or over		All	
	Freq	Pct	Freq	Pct	Freq	Pct	Freq	Pct
i	157	64.9	82	69.5	110	73.8	349	68.6
e	55	22.7	18	15.3	20	13.4	93	18.3
(omit)	12	5.0	13	11.0	4	2.7	29	5.7
a	5	2.1	1	0.8	2	1.3	8	1.6
o	2	0.8	0	0.0	1	0.7	3	0.6
y	2	0.8	0	0.0	1	0.7	3	0.6
ei	2	0.8	0	0.0	7	4.7	9	1.8
ie	2	0.8	1	0.8	0	0.0	2	0.4
ee	2	0.8	1	0.8	0	0.0	3	0.6
u	1	0.4	0	0.0	1	0.7	3	0.6
ch	1	0.4	0	0.0	0	0.0	1	0.2
oo	1	0.4	1	0.8	0	0.0	1	0.2
ii	0	0.0	0	0.0	2	1.3	3	0.6
ia	0	0.0	0	0.0	1	0.7	1	0.2
li	0	0.0	1	0.8	0	0.0	1	0.2
Totals	242	100.0	118	100.0	149	100.0	509	100.0

TABLE 3   *Phoneme: /e/*

Age: Spelling	Under 6		Unknown		6 or over		All	
	Freq	Pct	Freq	Pct	Freq	Pct	Freq	Pct
a	87	73.7	48	57.1	56	71.8	191	68.2
ay	13	11.0	14	16.7	2	2.6	29	10.4
ae	4	3.4	2	2.4	6	7.7	12	4.3
e	3	2.5	6	7.1	2	2.6	11	3.9
ai	3	2.5	3	3.6	3	3.8	9	3.2
(omit)	2	1.7	4	4.8	1	1.3	7	2.5
ey	2	1.7	2	2.4	0	0.0	4	1.4
y	1	0.8	2	2.4	4	5.1	7	2.5
auy	1	0.8	0	0.0	0	0.0	1	0.4
ol	1	0.8	0	0.0	0	0.0	1	0.4
eea	1	0.8	0	0.0	0	0.0	1	0.4
ee	0	0.0	1	1.2	1	1.3	2	0.7
ea	0	0.0	0	0.0	1	1.3	1	0.4
eay	0	0.0	1	1.2	0	0.0	1	0.4
aue	0	0.0	0	0.0	2	2.6	2	0.7
au	0	0.0	1	1.2	0	0.0	1	0.4
Totals	118	100.0	84	100.0	78	100.0	280	100.0

TABLE 4 *Phoneme /i/*

Age: Spelling	Under 6		Unknown		6 or over		All	
	Freq	Pct	Freq	Pct	Freq	Pct	Freq	Pct
e	100	46.5	59	38.8	62	48.4	221	44.6
y	36	16.7	43	28.3	34	26.6	113	22.8
(omit)	17	7.9	9	5.9	3	2.3	29	5.9
i	16	7.4	9	5.9	10	7.8	35	7.1
ey	14	6.5	2	1.3	1	0.8	17	3.4
ay	11	5.1	5	3.3	0	0.0	16	3.2
ee	10	4.7	11	7.2	5	3.9	26	5.3
a	5	2.3	0	0.0	1	0.8	6	1.2
ea	2	0.9	3	2.0	4	3.1	9	1.8
ei	1	0.5	0	0.0	0	0.0	1	0.2
ie	1	0.5	4	2.6	4	3.1	9	1.8
iee	1	0.5	1	0.7	0	0.0	2	0.4
eyi	1	0.5	0	0.0	0	0.0	1	0.2
oy	0	0.0	4	2.6	0	0.0	4	0.8
iey	0	0.0	1	0.7	0	0.0	1	0.2
as	0	0.0	0	0.0	1	0.8	1	0.2
ue	0	0.0	0	0.0	1	0.8	1	0.2
ye	0	0.0	0	0.0	2	1.6	2	0.4
eae	0	0.0	1	0.7	0	0.0	1	0.2
Totals	215	100.0	152	100.0	128	100.0	495	100.0

TABLE 5 *Phoneme: /ə/*

Age: Spelling	Under 6		Unknown		6 ot over		All	
	Freq	Pct	Freq	Pct	Freq	Pct	Freq	Pct
(omit)	86	28.6	37	24.0	45	19.7	168	24.6
i	83	27.6	32	20.8	67	29.4	182	26.6
e	39	13.0	29	18.8	58	25.4	126	18.4
o	34	11.3	7	4.5	17	7.5	58	8.5
a	26	8.6	22	14.3	27	11.8	75	11.0
u	25	8.3	16	10.4	9	3.9	50	7.3
l	3	1.0	6	3.9	2	0.9	11	1.6
ei	1	0.3	0	0.0	1	0.4	2	0.3
rl	1	0.3	0	0.0	0	0.0	1	0.1
ai	1	0.3	0	0.0	0	0.0	1	0.1
n	1	0.3	0	0.0	0	0.0	1	0.1
r	1	0.3	0	0.0	0	0.0	1	0.1
y	0	0.0	1	0.6	0	0.0	1	0.1
ap	0	0.0	0	0.0	1	0.4	1	0.1
ou	0	0.0	1	0.6	0	0.0	1	0.1
ee	0	0.0	2	1.3	0	0.0	2	0.3
eo	0	0.0	0	0.0	1	0.4	1	0.1
de	0	0.0	1	0.6	0	0.0	1	0.1
Totals	301	100.0	154	100.0	228	100.0	683	100.0

TABLE 6 *Phoneme:* /ŋ/

Age: Spelling	Under 6		Unknown		6 or over		All	
	Freq	Pct	Freq	Pct	Freq	Pct	Freq	Pct
n	33	37.5	9	18.7	8	13.1	50	25.4
g	23	26.1	9	18.7	3	4.9	35	17.8
(omit)	19	21.6	6	12.5	10	16.4	35	17.8
ng	11	12.5	19	39.6	37	60.7	67	34.0
v	1	1.1	0	0.0	0	0.0	1	0.5
de	1	1.1	1	2.1	0	0.0	2	1.0
ne	0	0.0	0	0.0	1	1.6	1	0.5
lin	0	0.0	1	2.1	0	0.0	1	0.5
gn	0	0.0	2	4.2	1	1.6	3	1.5
nin	0	0.0	0	0.0	1	1.6	1	0.5
nge	0	0.0	1	2.1	0	0.0	1	0.5
Totals	88	100.0	48	100.0	61	100.0	197	100.0

TABLE 7   *Phoneme:* /š/

Age: Spelling	Under 6		Unknown		6 or over		All	
	Freq	Pct	Freq	Pct	Freq	Pct	Freq	Pct
sh	16	42.1	8	50.0	20	69.0	44	53.0
s	7	18.4	7	43.8	2	6.9	16	19.3
h	4	10.5	0	0.0	0	0.0	4	4.8
ch	2	5.3	0	0.0	2	6.9	4	4.8
hc	2	5.3	0	0.0	0	0.0	2	2.4
ti	2	5.3	0	0.0	1	3.4	3	3.6
(omit)	1	2.6	0	0.0	0	0.0	1	1.2
sc	1	2.6	0	0.0	0	0.0	1	1.2
nd	1	2.6	0	0.0	0	0.0	1	1.2
hs	1	2.6	0	0.0	0	0.0	1	1.2
sht	1	2.6	0	0.0	0	0.0	1	1.2
th	0	0.0	0	0.0	3	10.3	3	3.6
tt	0	0.0	0	0.0	1	3.4	1	1.2
sch	0	0.0	1	6.3	0	0.0	1	1.2
Totals	38	100.0	16	100.0	29	100.0	83	100.0

TABLE 8   *Phoneme: /z/*

Age: Spelling	Under 6		Unknown		6 or over		All	
	Freq	Pct	Freq	Pct	Freq	Pct	Freq	Pct
s	92	82.1	59	72.0	88	85.4	239	80.5
z	5	4.5	6	7.3	0	0.0	11	3.7
(omit)	3	2.7	0	0.0	2	1.9	5	1.7
se	3	2.7	10	12.2	8	7.8	21	7.1
fs	2	1.8	2	2.4	3	2.9	7	2.4
c	1	0.9	3	3.7	0	0.0	4	1.3
is	1	0.9	0	0.0	0	0.0	1	0.3
x	1	0.9	0	0.0	0	0.0	1	0.3
zs	1	0.9	0	0.0	0	0.0	1	0.3
ses	1	0.9	0	0.0	0	0.0	1	0.3
zcs	1	0.9	0	0.0	0	0.0	1	0.3
su	1	0.9	0	0.0	0	0.0	1	0.3
ss	0	0.0	2	2.4	1	1.0	3	1.0
ese	0	0.0	0	0.0	1	1.0	1	0.3
Totals	112	100.0	82	100.0	103	100.0	297	100.0

TABLE 9   *Phoneme:* /ɝ/

Age: Spelling	Under 6 Freq	Pct	Unknown Freq	Pct	6 or over Freq	Pct	All Freq	Pct
r	75	59.1	37	56.1	49	63.6	161	59.6
er	31	24.4	11	16.7	15	19.5	57	21.1
or	6	4.7	3	4.5	2	2.6	11	4.1
(omit)	4	3.1	1	1.5	1	1.3	6	2.2
ir	4	3.1	10	15.2	1	1.3	15	5.6
ar	2	1.6	2	3.0	0	0.0	4	1.5
a	2	1.6	1	1.5	0	0.0	3	1.1
rb	1	0.8	0	0.0	0	0.0	1	0.4
e	1	0.8	0	0.0	2	2.6	3	1.1
ur	1	0.8	1	1.5	3	3.9	5	1.9
t	0	0.0	0	0.0	1	1.3	1	0.4
ei	0	0.0	0	0.0	1	1.3	1	0.4
ure	0	0.0	0	0.0	2	2.6	2	0.7
Totals	127	100.0	66	100.0	77	100.0	270	100.0

TABLE 10 *Phonemes: /əl/*

Age: Spelling	Under 6 Freq	Under 6 Pct	Unknown Freq	Unknown Pct	6 or over Freq	6 or over Pct	All Freq	All Pct
l	22	41.5	14	32.6	21	47.7	57	40.7
(omit)	5	9.4	1	2.3	0	0.0	6	4.3
el	4	7.5	6	14.0	6	13.6	16	11.4
ol	4	7.5	2	4.7	4	9.1	10	7.1
o	4	7.5	0	0.0	0	0.0	4	2.9
le	3	5.7	6	14.0	2	4.5	11	7.9
al	3	5.7	5	11.6	1	2.3	9	6.4
il	2	3.8	1	2.3	2	4.5	5	3.6
ll	1	1.9	0	0.0	1	2.3	2	1.4
ul	1	1.9	5	11.6	3	6.8	9	6.4
ule	1	1.9	1	2.3	0	0.0	2	1.4
all	1	1.9	0	0.0	1	2.3	2	1.4
ale	1	1.9	0	0.0	0	0.0	1	0.7
rl	1	1.9	0	0.0	0	0.0	1	0.7
ler	0	0.0	1	2.3	0	0.0	1	0.7
ell	0	0.0	0	0.0	0	0.0	1	0.7
ill	0	0.0	0	0.0	1	2.3	1	0.7
oul	0	0.0	1	2.3	1	2.3	1	0.7
eol	0	0.0	0	0.0	1	2.3	1	0.7
Totals	53	100.0	43	100.0	44	100.0	140	100.0

TABLE 11   *Phonemes: /əm/*

Age: Spelling	Under 6		Unknown		6 or over		All	
	Freq	Pct	Freq	Pct	Freq	Pct	Freq	Pct
m	3	33.3	0	0.0	1	14.3	4	23.5
em	2	22.2	0	0.0	0	0.0	2	11.8
am	2	22.2	0	0.0	0	0.0	2	11.8
umb	1	11.1	0	0.0	0	0.0	1	5.9
um	1	11.1	0	0.0	0	0.0	1	5.9
im	0	0.0	0	0.0	4	57.1	4	23.5
om	0	0.0	1	100.0	2	28.6	3	17.6
Totals	9	100.0	1	100.0	7	100.0	17	100.0

TABLE 12 *Phonemes:* /ən/

Age: Spelling	Under 6 Freq	Under 6 Pct	Unknown Freq	Unknown Pct	6 or over Freq	6 or over Pct	All Freq	All Pct
in	40	40.4	16	29.6	24	40.7	80	37.7
n	19	19.2	6	11.1	11	18.6	36	17.0
on	12	12.1	3	5.6	3	5.1	18	8.5
en	9	9.1	8	14.8	11	18.6	28	13.2
un	6	6.1	6	11.1	1	1.7	13	6.1
(omit)	5	5.1	2	3.7	1	1.7	8	3.8
an	3	3.0	3	5.6	3	5.1	9	4.2
i	2	2.0	1	1.9	0	0.0	3	1.4
e	1	1.0	1	1.9	0	0.0	2	0.9
it	1	1.0	0	0.0	0	0.0	1	0.5
n	1	1.0	0	0.0	0	0.0	1	0.5
yx	0	0.0	1	1.9	0	0.0	1	0.5
im	0	0.0	1	1.9	0	0.0	1	0.5
ine	0	0.0	0	0.0	1	1.7	1	0.5
ann	0	0.0	0	0.0	1	1.7	1	0.5
one	0	0.0	0	0.0	2	3.4	2	0.9
ne	0	0.0	1	1.9	0	0.0	1	0.5
a	0	0.0	2	3.7	0	0.0	2	0.9
ein	0	0.0	0	0.0	1	1.7	1	0.5
nt	0	0.0	1	1.9	0	0.0	1	0.5
den	0	0.0	1	1.9	0	0.0	1	0.5
id	0	0.0	1	1.9	0	0.0	1	0.5
Totals	99	100.0	54	100.0	59	100.0	212	100.0

TABLE 13   *Phonemes: /nt/*

Age: Spelling	Under 6 Freq	Pct	Unknown Freq	Pct	6 or over Freq	Pct	All Freq	Pct
nt	30	44.8	19	54.3	39	75.0	88	57.1
t	19	28.4	8	22.9	7	13.5	34	22.1
n	9	13.4	0	0.0	2	3.8	11	7.1
(omit)	4	6.0	2	5.7	1	1.9	7	4.5
nte	2	3.0	0	0.0	1	1.9	3	1.9
nd	1	1.5	1	2.9	1	1.9	3	1.9
tit	1	1.5	0	0.0	0	0.0	1	0.6
nch	1	1.5	0	0.0	0	0.0	1	0.6
xt	0	0.0	1	2.9	0	0.0	1	0.6
nc	0	0.0	1	2.9	0	0.0	1	0.6
ntu	0	0.0	0	0.0	1	1.9	1	0.6
m	0	0.0	1	2.9	0	0.0	1	0.6
te	0	0.0	1	2.9	0	0.0	1	0.6
t	0	0.0	1	2.9	0	0.0	1	0.6
Totals	67	100.0	35	100.0	52	100.0	154	100.0

TABLE 14 *Phonemes: /nd/*

Age: Spelling	Under 6		Unknown		6 or over		All	
	Freq	Pct	Freq	Pct	Freq	Pct	Freq	Pct
nd	24	60.0	18	78.3	19	76.0	61	69.3
d	9	22.5	3	13.0	1	4.0	13	14.8
n	2	5.0	1	4.3	1	4.0	4	4.5
(omit)	1	2.5	0	0.0	1	4.0	2	2.3
ne	1	2.5	0	0.0	0	0.0	1	1.1
m	1	2.5	0	0.0	0	0.0	1	1.1
dd	1	2.5	0	0.0	0	0.0	1	1.1
mw	1	2.5	0	0.0	0	0.0	1	1.1
nt	0	0.0	0	0.0	1	4.0	1	1.1
nde	0	0.0	0	0.0	2	8.0	2	2.3
nn	0	0.0	1	4.3	0	0.0	1	1.1
Totals	40	100.0	23	100.0	25	100.0	88	100.0

TABLE 15   *Phonemes: /mp/*

Age: Spelling	Under 6		Unknown		6 or over		All	
	Freq	Pct	Freq	Pct	Freq	Pct	Freq	Pct
mp	4	44.4	0	0.0	1	25.0	5	31.3
p	3	33.3	3	100.0	0	0.0	6	37.5
m	2	22.2	0	0.0	2	50.0	4	25.0
mpt	0	0.0	0	0.0	1	25.0	1	6.3
Totals	9	100.0	3	100.0	4	100.0	16	100.0

TABLE 16 *Phonemes: /mb/*

Age:	Under 6		Unknown		6 or over		All	
Spelling	Freq	Pct	Freq	Pct	Freq	Pct	Freq	Pct
mb	6	75.0	2	66.7	4	36.4	12	54.5
b	2	25.0	1	33.3	0	0.0	3	13.6
md	0	0.0	0	0.0	6	54.5	6	27.3
nd	0	0.0	0	0.0	1	9.1	1	4.5
Totals	8	100.0	3	100.0	11	100.0	22	100.0

TABLE 17 *Phonemes: /ŋk/*

Age: Spelling	Under 6		Unknown		6 or over		All	
	Freq	Pct	Freq	Pct	Freq	Pct	Freq	Pct
k	4	26.7	4	44.4	4	36.4	12	34.3
c	4	26.7	1	11.1	4	36.4	9	25.7
nc	3	20.0	0	0.0	0	0.0	3	8.6
nk	2	13.3	2	22.2	0	0.0	4	11.4
kce	1	6.7	0	0.0	0	0.0	1	2.9
q	1	6.7	0	0.0	1	9.1	1	2.9
ng	0	0.0	1	11.1	0	0.0	1	2.9
n	0	0.0	0	0.0	1	9.1	1	2.9
ngk	0	0.0	1	11.1	1	9.1	1	2.9
nl	0	0.0	1	11.1	0	0.0	1	2.9
(omit)	0	0.0	0	0.0	1	9.1	1	2.9
Totals	15	100.0	9	100.0	11	100.0	35	100.0

TABLE 18 *Phonemes:* /ŋg/

Age: Spelling	Under 6		Unknown		6 or over		All	
	Freq	Pct	Freq	Pct	Freq	Pct	Freq	Pct
g	8	66.7	1	20.0	0	0.0	9	47.4
ng	2	16.7	2	40.0	2	100.0	6	31.6
(omit)	1	8.3	0	0.0	0	0.0	1	5.3
ngw	1	8.3	0	0.0	0	0.0	1	5.3
ling	0	0.0	1	20.0	0	0.0	1	5.3
ngg	0	0.0	1	20.0	0	0.0	1	5.3
Totals	12	100.0	5	100.0	2	100.0	19	100.0

Bibliography

Beers, C. S. (1980), 'The relationship of cognitive development to spelling and reading abilities,' in E. H. Henderson and J. W. Beers (eds), *Developmental and Cognitive Aspects of Learning to Spell*, Newark, Del.: International Reading Association.

Beers, J. W. (1974), 'First and second grade children's developing orthographic concepts of tense and lax vowels' (doctoral dissertation, University of Virginia), *Dissertation Abstracts International*, 1975, *35*(08), 4972A (University Microfilms No. 75-4694).

Beers, J. W., Beers, C. S. and Grant, K. (1977), 'The logic behind children's spelling,' *Elementary School Journal*, *3*, 238-42.

Berko, J. (1958), 'The child's learning of English morphology,' *Word, 14*, 150-77.

Bissex. G. L. (1980), *GNYS AT WRK: A Child Learns to Write and Read*, Cambridge, Mass.: Harvard University Press.

Boiarsky, C. (1969), 'Consistency of spelling and pronunciation deviation of Appalachian students,' *Modern Language Journal, 53*, 347-50.

Bradley, L. and Bryant, P. E. (1978), 'Difficulties in auditory organization as a possible cause of reading backwardness,' *Nature, 271*, 746-7.

Britton, J. (1970), *Language and Learning*, Coral Gables, Fla.: University of Miami Press.

Bryant, P. E. and Bradley, L. (1980), 'Why children sometimes write words which they do not read,' in U. Frith (ed.), *Cognitive Processes in Spelling*, London: Academic Press.

Cahen, L. S., Craun, M. J. and Johnson, S. K. (1971), 'Spelling difficulty – a survey of the research,' *Review of Educational Research, 41*, 281-301.

Canfield, D. L. (1981), *Spanish Pronunciation in the Americas*, Chicago: The University of Chicago Press.

Castrup, K. H. (1978), 'Insights into acquisition of the written language, based upon the spontaneous writings of a first and second school year – synopsis,' paper presented at the IRA World Conference on Reading, Hamburg, West Germany (S. J. McCord, translator).

Chomsky, C. (1970), 'Reading, writing, and phonology,' *Harvard Educational Review*, XL, 287-309.

Chomsky, C. (1971), 'Write first, read later,' *Childhood Education*, March, 296-9.

Chomsky, C. (1975a), 'How sister got into the grog,' *Early Years*, November, 36-9, 77-9.

Chomsky, C. (1975b), 'Invented spelling in the open classroom,' *Word* (special issue: *Child Language Today*) 499-518.

Chomsky, C. (1979), 'Approaching reading through invented spelling,' in P. Weaver and L. B. Resnick (eds), *The Theory and Practice of Early Reading* (Vol. 2), Hillsdale, N.J.: Lawrence Erlbaum Associates.

Chomsky, N. and Halle, M. (1968), *The Sound Pattern of English*, New York: Harper & Row.

Chu-Chang, M. and Loritz, D. J. (1977), 'Phonological encoding of Chinese ideographs in short-term memory,' *Language Learning*, 27, 341-52.

Clay, M. M. (1975), *What Did I Write?*, London: Heinemann Educational Books.

Cronnell, B. (1982a), *Black-English Influences in the Writing of Third- and Sixth-Grade Black Students*, Southwest Regional Laboratory Technical Note, TN 2-82/12.

Cronnell, B. (1982b), *A Preliminary Study of Language Influences in the English Writing of Third- and Sixth-Grade Chicano Students*, Southwest Regional Laboratory Technical Note, TN 2-82/13.

Eichler, W. (1976), 'Zur linguistischen Fehleranalyse von Spontanschreibungen bei Vor- und Grundschulkindern,' in A. Hofer (ed.), *Lesenlernen: Theorie und Unterricht*, Düsseldorf: Pädagogischer Verlag Schwann.

Elkind, D. (1974), 'Cognitive development and reading,' paper presented at the annual meeting of the International Reading Association, New Orleans.

Farnham-Diggory, S. (1978), 'How to study reading: some information processing ways,' in F. B. Murray and J. J. Pikulski (eds), *The Acquisition of Reading: Cognitive, Linguistic, and Perceptual Prerequisites*, Baltimore: University Park Press.

Ferguson, C. A. (1971), 'Contrasting patterns of literacy acquisition in a multilingual nation,' in W. H. Whitley (ed.), *Language Use and Social Change*, London: Oxford University Press.

Ferreiro, E. (1978), 'What is written in a written sentence? A developmental answer,' *Journal of Education*, 160(4), 25-39.

Ferreiro, E. (1980), 'The relationship between oral and written language: the children's viewpoints,' paper presented at the preconvention institute, International Reading Association, St Louis, 6 May.

Ferreiro, E. and Teberosky, A. (1982), *Literacy before Schooling*, Exeter, New Hampshire: Heinemann Educational Books.

Fischer, K. W. (1980), 'A theory of cognitive development: the construction of hierarchies of skills,' *Psychological Review*, 87, 477-531.

Fisher, E. M. (1973), 'A linguistic investigation of first-grade children's spelling errors as they occur in their written compositions' (doctoral dissertation, University of Virginia), *Dissertation Abstracts International*, 1973, 34, 1480A (University Microfilms No. 73-25, 013).

Fox, S. E. and Allen, V. G. (1983), *The Language Arts: An Integrated Approach*, New York: Holt, Rinehart & Winston.

Frith, U. (1980), 'Unexpected spelling problems,' in U. Frith (ed.), *Cognitive Processes in Spelling*, London: Academic Press.

Gates, A. I. (1922), 'The psychology of reading and spelling,' in *Contributions to Education*, New York: Bureau of Publications, Teachers College, Columbia University.

Gates, A. I. (1926), 'A study of the role of visual perception, intelligence, and certain associative processes in reading and spelling,' *Journal of Educational Psychology*, 17, 433-45.

Gates, A. I. (1937), *A List of Spelling Difficulties in 3876 Words*, New York: Teachers College, Columbia University.

Gentry, J. R. (1977), 'A study of the orthographic strategies of beginning readers' (doctoral dissertation, University of Virginia), *Dissertation Abstracts International*, 1979. *39*(07), 4017A (University Microfilms No. 79-01-152).

Gentry, J. R. and Henderson, E. H. (1978), 'Three steps to teaching beginning readers to spell,' *The Reading Teacher*, March, 632-7.

Gerritz, K. E. (1974), 'First graders spelling of vowels: an exploratory study' (doctoral dissertation, Harvard University), *Dissertation Abstracts International*, 1975, *36*(06), 3506A (University Microfilms No. 75-26, 907).

Gill, C. E. (1980), 'An analysis of spelling errors in French' (doctoral dissertation, University of Virginia), *Dissertation Abstracts International*, 1981, *9*, 3924A (University Microfilms No. 80-26641).

Gleitman, L. R. and Gleitman, H. (1970), *Phrase and Paraphrase: Some Innovative Uses of Language*, New York: W. W. Norton.

Gleitman, L. R. and Rozin, P. (1977), 'The structure and acquisition of reading I: relations between orthographies and the structure of language,' in A. S. Reber and D. L. Scarborough (eds), *Toward a Psychology of Reading: The Proceedings of the CUNY Conference*, Hillsdale, N.J.: Lawrence Erlbaum Associates.

Goodman, K. S. (1969), 'Analysis of oral reading miscues: applied psycholinguistics,' *Reading Research Quarterly*, 5, 9-30.

Goodman, Y. M. and Altwerger, B. (1981), 'A study of the development of literacy in preschool children,' (occasional papers, Program in Language and Literaracy, Tuscon, Ariz.: Arizona Center for Research and Development), University of Arizona.

Goodman, Y. M. and Burke, C. L. (1972), *Reading Miscue Inventory Kit*, New York: The Macmillan Company.

Goodman, Y. M. and Goodman, K. S. (1963), 'Spelling ability of a self-taught reader,' *Elementary School Journal*, *64*, 149-54.

Graham, L. W. and House, A. S. (1971), 'Phonological oppositions in children: a perceptual study,' *Journal of the Acoustical Society of America*, *49*, 559-66.

Graham, R. T. and Rudorf, E. H. (1970),. 'Dialect and spelling,' *Elementary English*, *47*, 363-76.

Groff, P. (1973), 'Children's speech errors and their spelling,' *The*

Elementary School Journal, *73*(2), 88-96.

Hanna, P. R., Hanna, J. S., Hodges, R. E. and Rudorf, E. H. (1966), *Phoneme-Grapheme Correspondences as Cues to Spelling Improvement*, Washington, D.C.: U.S. Government Printing Office.

Henderson, E. H. and Beers, J. W. (eds) (1980), *Developmental and Cognitive Aspects of Learning to Spell*, Newark, Del.: International Reading Association.

Horn, E. (1919), 'Principles of method in teaching spelling as derived from scientific investigation,' in *Eighteenth Yearbook of the National Society for the Study of Education, Part II*, Bloomington, Ill.: Public School Publishing Company.

Kligman, D. and Cronnell, B. (1974), *Black English and Spelling* (Technical Report 50), (ERIC Document Reproduction Service No. ED 108 234).

Kligman, D., Cronnell, B. and Verna, G. B. (1972), 'Black English pronunciation and spelling performance,' *Elementary English*, 1247-53.

Klima, E. S. (1972), 'How alphabets might reflect language,' in J. F. Kavanagh and I. G. Mattingly (eds), *Language by Ear and by Eye*, Cambridge, Mass.: M.I.T. Press.

Knafle, J. D. (1973), 'Auditory perception of rhyming in kindergarten children,' *Journal of Speech and Hearing Research*, *16*, 482-7.

Kuo, W. (1978), 'A preliminary study of reading disabilities in the Republic of China,' paper by National Taiwan Normal University, Graduate School of Education, *20*, 57-78.

Kurath, H. and McDavid, R. I., Jr (1961), *The Pronunciation of English in the Atlantic States*, Ann Arbor: University of Michigan Press.

Kyöstiö, O. K. (1980), 'Is learning to read easy in a language in which the grapheme-phoneme correspondences are regular?' in J. F. Kavanagh and R. L. Venezky (eds), *Orthography, Reading, and Dyslexia*, Baltimore: University Park Press.

Labov, W. (1967), 'Some sources of reading problems for Negro speakers of nonstandard English,' in A. Frazier (ed.), *New Directions in Elementary English*, Champaign, Ill.: National Council of Teachers of English, 140-67. Reprinted in J. C. Baratz and R. W. Shuy (eds), *Teaching Black Children to Read*, Washington, D.C.: Center for Applied Linguistics Urban Language Series, 1969, 29-67.

Labov, W. (1972), *Sociolinguistic Patterns*, Philadelphia, Pa.: University of Pennsylvania Press.

Ladefoged, P. (1975), *A Course in Phonetics* (2nd edn), New York: Harcourt Brace Jovanovich.

Lavine, L. O. (1977), 'Differentiation of letterlike forms in prereading children,' *Developmental Psychology*, *13*(2), 89-94.

Léon, P. R. (1966), *Pronunciation du français standard*, Paris: Librairie Marcel Didier.

Liberman, I. Y., Liberman, A. M., Mattingly, I. and Shankweiler, D. (1980), 'Orthography and the beginning reader,' in J. F. Kavanagh and R. L. Venezky (eds), *Orthography, Reading, and Dyslexia*, Baltimore: University Park Press.

Liberman, I. Y., Shankweiler, D., Fischer, F. W. and Carter, B. (1974),

'Explicit syllable and phoneme segmentation in the young child,' *Journal of Experimental Child Psychology*, *18*, 201-12.

Liberman, I. Y., Shankweiler, D., Liberman, A. M., Fowler, C. and Fisher, F. W. (1977), 'Phonetic segmentation and recoding in the beginning reader,' in A. S. Reber and D. Scarborough (eds), *Toward a Psychology of Reading: The Proceedings of the CUNY Conference*, Hillsdale, N.J.: Lawrence Erlbaum Associates.

Makita, K. (1968), 'The rarity of reading disability in Japanese children,' *American Journal of Orthopsychiatry*, *38*, 599-614.

Malecot, A. (1960), 'Vowel nasality as a distinctive feature in American English,' *Language*, *36*, 222-9.

Marcel, T. (1980), 'Phonological awareness and phonological representation: investigation of a specific spelling problem,' in U. Frith (ed.), *Cognitive Processes in Spelling*, London: Academic Press.

Marino, J. (1978), 'Children's use of phonetic, graphemic, and morphophonemic cues in a spelling task' (doctoral dissertation, State University of New York-Albany), *Dissertation Abstracts International*, 1979, *39*(10), 5997A (University Microfilms No. 79-07220).

Marsh, G., Friedman, M., Welch, V. and Desberg, P. (1980), 'The development of strategies in spelling,' in U. Frith (ed.), *Cognitive Processes in Spelling*, London: Academic Press.

Marsh, G., Friedman, M. Welch, V. and Desberg, P. (1981), 'A cognitive developmental theory of reading acquisition,' in G. E. MacKinnon and T. G. Waller (eds), *Reading Research: Advances in Theory and Practice* (Vol. 3), New York: Academic Press.

Mater, E. (ed.) (1970), *Rucklaufiges Wörterbuch der deutschen Gegenwartssprache*, Leipzig: Veb Verlag Enzyklopadie.

Mayhew, D. C. (1977), 'An investigation to determine factors affecting selected kindergarten children's invented spelling' (doctoral dissertation, University of Georgia), *Dissertation Abstracts International*, 1978, *38*, 3998A (University Microfilms No. 77-29788).

Mendenhall, J. E. (1930a), *An Analysis of Spelling Errors*, New York: Teachers College Press, Columbia University.

Mendenhall, J. E. (1930b), 'The characteristics of spelling errors,' *Journal of Educational Psychology*, *21*, 648-56.

Montessori, M. (1964), *The Montessori Method*, New York: Schocken Books.

Morais, J., Cary, L., Alegria, J. and Bertelson, P. (1979), 'Does awareness of speech as a sequence of phones arise spontaneously?' *Cognition*, *7*, 323-31.

Morehead, D. M. (1971), 'Processing of phonological sequences by young children and adults,' *Child Development*, *42*, 279-89.

Niski, J. A. (1978), 'Nasal omissions in children's spelling,' unpublished manuscript, Instituut voor Algemene Taalwetenschap, Katholieke Universiteit, Nijmegen, Netherlands.

Olmsted, D. L. (1971), *Out of the Mouth of Babes: Earliest Stages in Language Learning*, The Hague: Mouton.

O'Neal, V. and Trabasso, T. (1976), 'Is there a correspondence between sound and spelling? Some implications for Black English speakers,' in

D. S. Harrison and T. Trabasso (eds), *Black English: A Seminar*, Hillsdale, N.J.: Lawrence Erlbaum Associates.

Paul, R. (1976), 'Invented spelling in kindergarten,' *Young Children*, *21*(3), 195-200.

Read, C. (1970), 'Children's perceptions of the sounds of English: phonology from three to six,' unpublished doctoral dissertation, Harvard University.

Read, C. (1971), 'Preschool children's knowledge of English phonology,' *Harvard Educational Review*, *41*, 1-34.

Read, C. (1975), *Children's Categorizations of Speech Sounds in English*, Urbana, Ill.: National Council of Teachers of English.

Read, C. (1980), 'Creative spelling by young children,' in T. Shopen and J. M. Williams, (eds), *Standards and Dialects in English*, Cambridge, Mass.: Winthrop Publishers.

Read, C. (1981), 'Writing is not the inverse of reading for young children,' in C. H. Frederiksen and J. F. Dominic (eds), *Writing: The Nature, Development, and Teaching of Written Communication* (Vol. 2), Hillsdale, N.J.: Lawrence Erlbaum Associates.

Read, C., Zhang, Y., Nie, H. and Ding, B. (forthcoming), 'The ability to manipulate speech sounds depends on knowing alphabetic spelling.'

Rosen, C. and Rosen, H. (1973), *The Language of Primary School Children*, Harmondsworth, England: Penguin Education.

Rozin, P. and Gleitman, L. R. (1977), 'The structure and acquisition of reading II: the reading process and the acquisition of the alphabetic principle,' in A. S. Reber and D. L. Scarborough (eds), *Toward a Psychology of Reading: The Proceedings of the CUNY Conference*, Hillsdale, N.J.: Lawrence Erlbaum Associates.

Rozin, P., Poritsky, S. and Stotsky, R. (1971), 'American children with reading problems can easily learn to read English represented by Chinese characters,' *Science*, *171*, 1264-7.

Sakamoto, T. (1980), 'Reading of Hiragana,' in J. F. Kavanagh and R. L. Venezky (eds), *Orthography, Reading and Dyslexia*, Baltimore: University Park Press.

Sapir, E. (1925), 'Sound patterns in language,' *Language*, *1*, 37-51.

Sinclair, A., Jarvella, R. and Levelt, W. J. M. (eds) (1978), *The Child's Conception of Language*, Berlin: Springer Verlag.

Singh, S. and Woods, D. R. (1971), 'Perceptual structure of 12 American English vowels,' *Journal of the Acoustical Society of America*, *49*, 1861-6.

Staczek, J. J. (1982), 'Expanded subcategorization of Spanish-English bilingual spelling strategies,' in J. A. Fishman and G. D. Keller (eds), *Bilingual Education for Hispanic Students in the United States*, New York: Teachers College Press, Columbia University.

Staczek, J. J. and Aid, F. M. (1981), 'Hortographia himortal: Spelling problems among bilingual students,' in G. Valdes, A. G. Lozano, and R. Garcia-Moya (eds), *Teaching Spanish to the Hispanic Bilingual: Issues, Aims, and Methods*, New York: Teachers College Press, Columbia University.

Stever, E. F. (1976), 'Dialectic and socioeconomic factors affecting the spelling strategies of second-grade students' (doctoral dissertation,

University of Virginia), *Dissertation Abstracts International*, 1977, *37*, 4120A (University Microfilms No. 77-149).

Sullivan, R. E. (1971), 'A comparison of certain relationships among selected phonological differences and spelling derivations for a group of Negro and a group of White second grade children' (doctoral dissertation, The University of Texas at Austin), *Dissertation Abstracts International*, 1972, *32*(11), 6300A (University Microfilms No. 72-15841).

Temple, C. A. (1978). 'An analysis of spelling errors in Spanish' (doctoral dissertation, University of Virginia), *Dissertation Abstracts International*, 1979, *2*, 721A (University Microfilms No. 79-16258).

Temple, C. (1980), 'Learning to spell in Spanish,' in M. L. Kamil and A. J. Moe (eds), *Perspectives on Reading Research and Instruction, 29th Yearbook of the National Reading Conference*, Washington, D.C.: The National Reading Conference, 172-8.

Temple, C., Nathan, R. and Burris, N. (1982), *The Beginnings of Writing*, Boston: Allyn and Bacon, Inc.

Temple, C. A., Schlicht, R. and Henderson, E. (1981), 'Invented spelling of German-speaking children,' paper presented to the McGuffey Reading Center Conference on the Virginia Spelling Studies, Charlottesville, Va., 1981.

Terrell, T. D. (1977), 'Universal constraints on variably deleted final consonants: evidence from Spanish,' *Canadian Journal of Linguistics*, 22, 157-8.

Thorndike, R. L. and Lorge, I. (1944), *The Teacher's Word Book of 30,000 Words*, New York: Teachers College, Columbia University.

Treiman, R. (1982), 'Children's and adults' classifications of stops after /s/,' paper presented at the Seventh Annual Boston University Conference on Language Development, Boston, Mass., Oct.

Treiman, R. (1983), 'Phonetic aspects of first graders' creative spellings of consonants,' paper presented at the Eighth Annual Boston University Conference on Language Development, Boston, Mass., 7-9 Oct.

Treiman, R. (in press), 'Phonemic analysis, spelling, and reading: the case of initial consonant clusters,' in T. Carr (ed.), *New Directions in Child Development: The Development of Reading Stills*, San Francisco: Jossey-Bass.

Treiman, R. and Baron, J. (1981), 'Segmental analysis ability: development and relation to reading ability,' in G. E. MacKinnon and T. G. Waller (eds), *Reading Research: Advances in Theory and Practice* (Vol. 3), New York: Academic Press.

Treiman, R. A., Baron, J. and Luk, K. (1981), 'Speech recoding in silent reading: a comparison of Chinese and English,' *Journal of Chinese Linguistics*, *9*, 116-25.

Tzeng, O. and Hung, D. (1980), 'Reading in a nonalphabetic writing system, some experimental studies,' in J. F. Kavanagh and R. L. Venezky (eds), *Orthography, Reading, and Dyslexia*, Baltimore: University Park Press.

Tzeng, O. J. L., Hung, D. L. and Wang, W. S-Y. (1977), 'Speech recoding in reading Chinese characters,' *Journal of Experimental Psychology: Human Learning and Memory*, *3*, 621-30.

van Heuven, V. J. (1980), 'Aspects of Dutch orthography and reading,' in J. F. Kavanagh and R. L. Venezky (eds), *Orthography, Reading, and Dyslexia*, Baltimore: University Park Press.

van Rijnsoever, R. (1979), 'Spellingen van voorschoolse kinderen en eersteklassers,' *Gramma: Nijmeegs tijdschrift voor taalkunde, 3*, 169-96.

Venezky, R. L. (1967), 'English orthography: its graphical structure and its relation to sound,' *Reading Research Quarterly, II*(3), 75-105.

Venezky, R. L. (1970), *The Structure of English Orthography*, The Hague: Mouton.

Venezky, R. L. (1971), 'The asymmetry of sound substitutions,' *ASHA, 13*, 538 (abstract).

Venezky, R. L. (1980), 'From Webster to Rice to Roosevelt, the formative years for spelling instruction and spelling reform in the U.S.A.' in U. Frith (ed.), *Cognitive Processes in Spelling*, London: Academic Press.

Weijnen, A. (1966), *Nederlandse Dialectkunde*, Assen: van Gorcum, N.V.

Wolff, Sister M. R. (1952), 'A study of spelling errors with implications concerning pertinent teaching methods,' *Elementary School Journal, 52*, 458-66.

Wolfram, W. and Fasold, R. W. (1974), *The Study of Social Dialects in American English*, New York: Prentice-Hall, Inc.

Zifcak, M. (1977), 'Phonological awareness and reading acquisition in first grade children' (doctoral dissertation, University of Connecticut), *Dissertation Abstracts International*, 1978, *38*(11), 6655A-6656A (University Microfilms No. 78-6156).

Zutell, J. (1980), 'Children's spelling strategies and their cognitive development,' in E. H. Henderson and J. W. Beers (eds), *Developmental and Cognitive Aspects of Learning to Spell*, Newark, Del.: International Reading Association.

Zutell, J. B., Jr (1975), 'Spelling strategies of primary school children and their relationship to the Piagetian concept of decentration' (doctoral dissertation, University of Virginia), *Dissertation Abstracts International*, 1975, *36*(08), 5030A (University Microfilms No. 76-18).

Index